Paul Terence

GUITAR BOOK

FOR ADULT BEGINNERS:
Learn to Play Guitar in 45 Hours

How to Play Guitar Chords, Strumming, Fingerstyle and Songs

+ Video & Audio Lessons

Messages about typos, errors, inaccuracies and suggestions for improving the quality are gratefully received at:
paulterenceinc@gmail.com

CONTENTS

CHAPTER 1

CHAPTER 2

CHAPTER 3

CHAPTER 4

MUSICAL RHYTHM:

CHAPTER 5

SONGS:

PSYCHOLOGY OF LEARNING TO PLAY GUITAR

PSY.1

Why it is important to learn by reading and doing the exercises in each chapter of this book step by step

Let's figure out what happens if you skip chapters and exercises, and what happens if you do everything step-by-step, as well as how to achieve the results you want quickly.

By reading the examples and following all the teaching instructions in this book, you will learn the skills easily and quickly. You will understand how to move your hands, how to place your fingers, how to produce the desired and beautiful sound, how to pinch a chord, and how to play a song.

If you skip chapters, you'll end up learning some guitar skills very poorly. For example, if you skip the topic of setting goals for learning, you may have less motivation to learn since you might not realize what you really want to play guitar for. If you skip the topic of "How to learn 2, 3, 5, 10 or more times faster", the learning process will be slower, and if you also criticize yourself for making mistakes, the learning will be much slower.

If you skip the topic of how to sit down with the guitar and immediately pick up the guitar the wrong way, it is highly possible that this will lead to back tension, neck tension, arterial compression in the neck, and possible headaches. If you skip the chapter of "tuning the guitar with a clip-on tuner", the guitar will be out of tune and then there will be a nasty sound. But usually a beginner with a poorly developed tuneful ears will not even hear that the guitar is out of tune. Then, when playing a out of tune guitar, a false sense of music will develop, which will eventually lead to more difficulties in singing and picking up music by ear in the future. And so on for each chapter.

I have a very amusing story about this topic. I've been writing this book's content for over 1 year and just before Christmas, in 2023, two new acquaintances I met at a business event came to visit me. They are two friends and two business partners, and they are completely opposite to each other in temperament. The first one does everything clearly by steps, step 1, step 2, step 3, step 4, step 5, etc., and he is a man of procedure. And the second is very chaotic, he does things as they occur to him, he does what comes into his head and thinks like a man of result.

We were sitting and talking. One of them saw a guitar on my wall and asked me if I play guitar. I said yes and played them a few songs. They really liked the way I play and said they would like to learn to play too. At that moment I had some printed materials of the book on the table next to me and they saw the materials. I told them I was writing a guitar teaching book.

They were interested and asked when the book would be ready. I told them that almost all the materials were ready, about 97% complete. The second one looked at the first one and with a defiant face said to him, "I bet I can learn to play guitar faster?" The first one said to him, "You bet." And so an interesting argument ensued. They bet that each will play 1 hour a day and in 1 month they will compare who plays better, on the example of playing a few songs. I sent them the book's materials and they each started learning to play for 1 hour a day.

After 1 month they visited me and we started comparing their playing on the songs We Wish You A Merry Christmas, All Through the Night and Buffalo Gals. The first one, who did all the tasks in the book step by step, played all 3 songs pretty easily. The second, was a little stressed because he could barely transpose just 2 chords in the Buffalo Gals song. We Wish You A Merry Christmas and All Through the Night he couldn't play because they have more chords in them. In the end, it turned out that the second skipped the chapter on learning psychology, skipped the chapter on hand placement, skipped the chapter on strumming, skipped the chapter on rhythm and started learning by playing these 3 songs. Naturally he learned to hold the guitar with his shoulders hunched over and neck tension. He twisted his left arm to set chords and with his right hand he learned to play fingerstyle with a bent brush. It was a telling example of the importance of learning consistently, step by step. His "results" temperament is useful in other contexts, such as in business, where he is thinking about point B and his partner is thinking about how to arrive at point B. But in training it is important to be in the process rather than the result, taking step by step sequential actions.

After we did an assessment of who learned to play better, both of them started taking guitar lessons from me. The hardest part was retraining the other to play correctly. It took us over 15 hours of lessons for him to learn how to sit correctly, put his hands on the guitar correctly, put chords correctly, play the strumming and fingerstyle. In fact, I just started teaching him from the beginning, right from this book's material. First we learned psychological techniques to make learning easier. Then we learned how to tune the guitar, how to sit down with the guitar, and hand placement on the guitar. He did all the exercises sequentially, step by step. Then we learned how to play the beat, then the rhythm and then we moved on to playing songs. In the end I taught him how to play correctly and he was able to play songs easily when he already had all the skills he needed to play songs.

You can skip chapters, then the learning will be sluggish, you'll probably learn some skills in a distorted way, which will lead to muscle strain and eventually dozens of hours of re-learning how to do it right, but if you want to learn for fun, so that you get it fast, it's cool if you:
1. Read each topic in sequence
2. Do exercises at the end of each topic, if there are exercises in it
3. Do exercises for as long as described in the topic.

On some topics you might think "I already know that," then I recommend asking yourself the question. "Am I doing this perfectly or at least well?" If not, then practice.

So let's study consistently and do all the tasks!

 **PSY.2**

Setting learning objectives

Let's talk about why it's important to have a clear goal in learning to play guitar.

If you set a goal correctly and clearly, it will be extremely easy to reach it. You'll be able to set the right path to get there as quickly, easily, and enjoyably as possible. You will understand what you are learning to play for and this understanding will motivate you to learn.

If you skip goal setting, there may be little motivation to learn because you may not realize what you really want to play guitar for.

When I was studying psychological techniques on personal effectiveness I came up with a technique for goal setting. I went to a room where I could be alone and sat in a chair. I imagined I was sitting in a movie theater. I imagined that in front of me within arm's length the center of the screen, which was as wide and high as my height. On the screen, I imagined I was watching a movie about my ideal self in the future, where I played guitar as much as I wanted to. I watched myself performing on stage with my music band. Bright lights illuminate me in the center of the stage and I play a guitar solo. My face is happy and satisfied. I'm acting out my guitar playing, and it looks awesome! The audience is in a positive mood, shouting my name and applauding me. After the concert I take pictures with the audience, give them autographs, chat with them. Then satisfied I go to the dressing room, sit on a chair to look at myself in the mirror and say how happy and happy I am to live the life I dream of. My partner in the music business comes up to me and tells me that he transferred $30,000 dollars to my bank account for the concert. I smile, imagining how I will spend this money on charity, on vacation, how I will take my mom and dad to the best restaurant. How my wife and I will go on vacation to a cozy beach.

Another day I practice my songs in my music studio, play AC/DC songs, Metallica songs, play Bach on guitar, play Vivaldi on guitar, play songs by Sting, The Beatles, Pink Floyd, Madonna, Led Zeppelin, Michael Jackson, Bee Gees, ZZ Top and many others....

Then I imagined the main character of the movie telling me why he started playing guitar. He said that he really liked listening to different music and he wanted not just to listen to it, but to learn how to play it. He wanted to learn different skills and improve every day, getting better and better. He wanted to evoke emotions in the audience, he wanted people to come to his concerts, he wanted to be noticed in new companies. Every time he picks up a guitar he instantly remembers what he plays guitar for and his motivation to play gets bigger and bigger.

And so on...

I imagined this "movie" for over an hour, picturing all the scenes and sounds in detail.

You can skip the goal setting and then your motivation to learn will be small, because you may not realize what you really want to play guitar for. But if you want to play the guitar with a high, to be always motivated to learn, then we go to the technique.

The technique of "seeing the future"

Imagine that you are sitting in a movie theater and watching a movie about yourself in the future. In front of you at arm's length distance is the center of a large screen, the width and height equal to your height. All you can see is this screen. The picture on the screen is very clear, bright, colorful, contrast and saturated. You are watching a movie about yourself in the future, where you already know how to play the guitar as you want.

1. Where are you in this movie, what and who is around you? What emotions do you see on your face? What emotions do you see on other people's faces, if any, in the movie?
2. Where else are you in this movie in a different place? What and who is around you? What emotions do you see on your face? What emotions do you see on other people's faces, if any, in the movie?
3. Where else are you in this movie in a different place? What and who is around you? What emotions do you see on your face? What emotions do you see on other people's faces, if any, in the movie?
4. Where else are you located...?
5. What songs do you play? (think of all the songs you want to play). What is your face like when you play each song?
6. Imagine that the main character of the movie (you in the future) tells you (the viewer) why he started playing guitar. Tells you what motivated him and motivates him to play guitar.

When you have watched a movie about yourself in the future you can write down on paper (or digitally) the answers to the questions that the main character (you from the future) told you.

It may happen that you are having a noisy time around you. Then you can go to a quiet place to do this exercise.

So settle in and start watching a movie about yourself in the future!

 **PSY.3**

What result will be after 45 hours of learning from this book

By practicing 1.5 hours every day for 30 days (or 1 hour a day for 45 days) and following all the instructions in this book, you can learn the basic techniques of strumming and fingerstyle, learn the basic open chords (A, Am, C, D, Dm, E, Em, G) and their transpositions, and learn to play 5-15 simple well-known songs. This will allow you to play almost any song in a simplified form. Further you will already improve your playing level and master new guitar skills.

 **PSY.4**

What to do if you want to sing while playing guitar

If you take singing lessons with a teacher, your vocal cords will be healthy. You will learn how to use your breathing muscles properly for a beautiful and ringing voice.

If you study on your own, and just shout as you can, then there is a high probability of damaging the vocal cords and then the voice will be croaky and is probable that it will stay that way forever.

There are 2 main types of singing. Pop vocals and academic vocals. They are completely different and if you want to sing, for example, as an opera singer, while going to a rock vocal teacher, you will get the exact opposite effect! Or vice versa, if you want to sing like a brutal rocker while going to an opera vocal teacher, you'll get the exact opposite.

You can do vocal training on your own, but then you have to remember the risk of injuring your vocal cords if you don't know how and what to do correctly. But if you want your voice to be beautiful and healthy, you quickly learn to sing, then decide what kind of vocal you want to sing and then find a vocal teacher.

If you don't realize how you want to sing, then listen to different genres of music and note for yourself what you like the most.

My fingers get tired when playing

While playing guitar, many small muscles in the palm of your hand work together with the muscles in your forearm that move your fingers. The finger muscles get tired because they are very small. They need time to get accustomed to it.

Look at how many muscles are in the palm of your hand and they all need to adapt to playing the guitar.

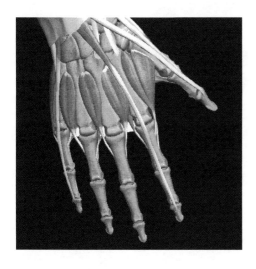
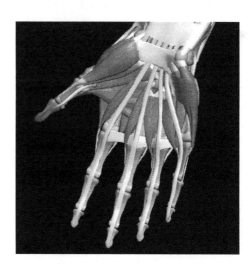

If you exercise for at least 1 hour every day, after 1-2 weeks your muscles will adapt and it will be much easier.

PSY.6

Tight skin thickening on the fingertips

Just like the small muscles of the palm and fingers, the skin on the fingertips of most people's hands is very soft. But when regular exposure (friction) in the same place on the skin begins, the skin starts to become rough - this is a body adaptation. If it wasn't, the skin would be worn down to the bone with constant exposure, but because it is compacted, it can easily withstand friction. So every time you play the guitar, you will stimulate the skin on your fingertips to become thicker.

Your fingertips may be a little sore for the first time (1-3 weeks).

VERY IMPORTANT: If you feel pain, it is best to rest for a couple of hours and return to playing. If necessary, rest more.

After 3-4 weeks of regular, daily practice, your fingertips will become tight and you will feel comfortable playing.

It is important that if you take regular breaks of 3-5 days during the initial training, you will prevent the formation of calluses on your fingers, because the skin starts to get rough when stimulated, and returns to its normal state when not stimulated. And since your skin is still soft, it is important to stimulate it regularly. So it is really important to play preferably every day.

It is important, if your palms were in water for a long time (shower, bath, swimming pool...) and the skin on your fingers got wet, it is very important to wait for complete drying and skin recovery (20-40 minutes) and only then play the guitar! If you start playing with soaked seals, the calluses can rip off the skin, leading to pain and healing for about a week. And the whole time this area will be sore.

Guitar types and how to choose the TYPE of guitar

We'll talk about the differences between guitars, what guitar you need and how to determine which guitar to choose.

If you choose the right guitar at the beginning of your training, once you have mastered the basic universal guitar skills, you can start learning to play songs in the music styles you like on a guitar that is designed for that purpose. If you initially buy a guitar that suits your needs, you will save more than $200, because the guitar you have will be enough.

If you choose a guitar of a type that is contrary to your objectives, you will have to purchase a new guitar, spend money and time on it, or play the wrong guitar and suffer from difficulty in playing.

GUITARS COME IN 3 TYPES:

| Classical guitar | Acoustic guitar | Electric guitar |

Classical (flamenco) guitar

It is used to play flamenco and classical music. This guitar has nylon strings that have a light tension and sound soft. It is played with the pads of the fingertips, but is most often played with the fingernails. Guitarists grow the nails on their right hand from 3mm to 1cm long and sharpen the nails in a special way.

To play hard rock, bardic songs, especially heavy metal on such a guitar will be extremely strange and sound bad. The tension of nylon strings is weak, so it is very comfortable for fingers to play.

There are no strap mounts on a classical guitar to play standing up. It is mostly played sitting down. The guitar sounds gentle, soft and romantic. It has a hollow (resonator) inside the body to amplify the volume of the sound. The guitar is lightweight because it is empty inside.

Acoustic guitar

The guitar has a metal rod inside the fingerboard to keep it intact and not break in half. The guitar has metal strings with a strong tension.

The sound of the guitar is ringing and loud. You can play almost any genre of music on it. Even flamenco and classical music will sound good. Hard rock ballads, blues, jazz sound great on an acoustic guitar. There is a variety of acoustic guitars that have a pickup, such a guitar can be connected to a combo amplifier and played through audio speakers. Sound effects can be added to a guitar plugged into a combo amp, making the electro-acoustic guitar very versatile. The guitar often has a cutout in the lower part of the guitar where the fingerboard is attached to the body so that you can play high notes, giving you more performance options. The guitar has a strap attachment for playing standing up.

An acoustic (or electro-acoustic) guitar is the perfect choice for learning! It will be easy to switch to an electric guitar after such a guitar.

An acoustic guitar has a hollow (resonator) inside the body to amplify the volume of the sound. It is slightly heavier in weight than a classical guitar.

Electric guitar

You can play anything on a guitar like this. It is absolutely universal. Due to the connection to an amplifier you can customize almost any sound, in some cases even the sound of a piano or violin.

The body of the electric guitar is solid and there is no resonator. Because of this, it is the heaviest of all types of guitars. If you start learning to play electric guitar right away, it will be much harder to learn.

The electric guitar has a complicated string arrangement (adjusting the fingerboard bend, string height, string length). This is unnecessary for a beginner. The main reason why it is more difficult to learn on it is that electric guitars have strings closer together than many acoustic guitars and classical guitars. This is done in order to play with a plectrum (a device used to pluck the strings). Because of this, it's harder for a beginner to properly place their fingers on the electric guitar without hitting neighboring strings. Plus, playing with a plectrum is much more difficult than playing with your fingers, because it requires more additional skills.

You can start right away with an electric guitar, but know that you won't be as easy to learn as an acoustic guitar.

It's better to start learning with an acoustic guitar and then switch to an electric guitar. This transition will be easy and comfortable for you.

Standard guitars are right-handed. It may happen that you are left-handed. Then you have options:

1. Learn to play like a right-handed player.
2. Buy a left-handed guitar. In this case you will have to mirror all the parts, because they are recorded with right-handed playing in mind.

Pick a guitar that suits your goals!

What to do if your fingers hurt from playing

For a beginner you need 8 or 9 string gauge. Usually in stores they install 11 gauge strings on acoustic guitar, they are very thick strings with very strong tension. Even I can hardly strum chords on these strings. And if the guitar is of poor quality, then playing it will be just a terrible torment, because on cheap acoustic guitars the strings are located very high above the metal strips on the neck. In order to clamp the strings you will have to put a lot of pressure on them. But even if a person has enough strength to clamp the strings, the sound will be false because of the fact that there is too strong change in the length of the string when pressing. That's why it is better to buy a good guitar at once and ask the seller in the music store to help pick up strings of 8 or 9 gauge specifically for your guitar.

 **PSY.9**

How to learn 2, 3, 5 or more times faster

Let's talk about the way that will allow you to learn many times faster in any sphere, including learning to play the guitar, as well as feel pleasant emotions from learning.

Every time you have done an action and you want to repeat it again, as well as to do this action even better and better, it is important for each action to provide positive reinforcement with a word, a phrase, a gesture or a nod of the head. This way the brain gets positive emotions and realizes that it is worth repeating the action again. This speeds up the learning process many times over. Most importantly, when you remember what you did, you reinforce the pattern of behavior you are reinforcing because you are remembering something you want to do again. It's like memorizing a text. The more times you repeat the text, the better you memorize it. It's the same thing here. The more you repeat in your imagination the actions you want to do, the better they are memorized. And when you reinforce yourself for actions in a positive state, that state is transferred to the actions you are reinforcing. You end up with a clearer, more vivid and detailed pattern of behavior that you reinforce with positive reinforcement + that behavior has a cool, positive state!

If you skip positive reinforcement for behaviors that you want to repeat, you are much less likely to repeat those behaviors. And if you did the actions in a negative state, when you repeat those actions, it's almost 100% that you'll do those actions in the same negative state as last time. Eventually you will stop doing it altogether and do something else.

Imagine you're walking through a door in a store and the person behind you asks you to hold the door for him. You hold the door for him and he silently walks past you and looks somewhere else with a neutral face.

Imagine you're walking into the same store again and again the same person asks you to hold the door for him. You hold the door for him and again he silently walks past you with a poker face.

Imagine the 3rd time you meet this person again at the entrance and he asks you to hold the door for him. You hold the door for him, and he ignores you again, like he's alone and you don't even exist.

So you meet this person for the fourth time. Are you gonna hold the door for him? Maybe you already want to ignore his request and mind your own business for the 2nd or 3rd time. This happens because there is no positive reinforcement for your actions.

I remember when I was learning to play chords on the guitar, I was listening to a psychology program on TV. They were talking about positive reinforcement. The program showed statistics of three groups of students in which they conducted a 1 month long experiment. In the first group of students, while studying, doing homework and doing exercises, teachers specifically told students negative words and reacted negatively to students' actions.

In the second group the teachers did not react in any way to the students' successes.

And in the third group, the teachers were always ONLY positively reinforcing the students.

The outcome was like this. After 1 month in the 1st group where negative reactions were said and done, the students' average score dropped from a B to a D.

In group 2, the average score dropped from a B to a B-.

And in group 3, EXACTLY where positive reinforcement was given to students' progress, the score went from a B to an A! Moreover, in this group, students became more cheerful, happier, some students quit their habits of playing computer games and drinking alcohol.

When the experiment ended, after 4 weeks, all 3 groups returned to the same scores they had before the experiment.

Then I got the idea to try positive reinforcement and started doing it every day over 200 times. Every hour I set my alarm clock and when it rang I would remember what I had done for the past hour and give myself 25 thanks for what I had done well for the past hour.

For example:
- I thought I wanted to play the guitar - *oh, that's so cool!*
- I shifted into a positive mood before picking up the guitar. *That's cool!*
- I stretched out my hands by squeezing a soft hand expander - *cool, now my fingers will move more easily on the neck of the guitar.*
- I sat down with a straight back to play the guitar. *Great!*
- I put a mirror in front of me to monitor the correct position of my body when playing the guitar - *great!*
- I was able to play a chord on the 3rd time - *great!*
- And now I was able to play a chord on the 2nd time - *great!*
- And so on, noting every little thing.

After the first day, when I made over 200 positive reinforcements to myself, already in the evening I felt like I had lived not 1 day but a whole super cool and positive week, because I had picked up on so many small details of my actions during that day. I accomplished **so much** in that day, that's how cool it was! And the mood at the end of the day was just great!

- After a week of daily positive reinforcement of myself when playing guitar, I noticed that I started learning much faster, I wanted to practice more often and longer and playing the guitar became much more enjoyable!!!

Since then, every day I pay attention to what I have done well and reinforce it with either a complimentary phrase (out loud or to myself), a head nod, a gesture or a smile.

I do the same thing in teaching my students by positively reinforcing their actions in learning.

You can skip this chapter and go straight to learning. Then the learning will be much slower. If you want to learn several times faster and feel really cool, then skip to the instructions.

I highly recommend you print out / rewrite the instructions and place them in a prominent place near your guitar so you always remember and apply positive reinforcement.

Instruction:
1. Choose any method of positive reinforcement. You can use different ways.
   - Gesture (everyone has a gesture that they consciously or unconsciously use in life when they are trying to achieve something. It can be a thumbs up 👍, OK 👌, victory pose ... head nod)...
   - Say any phrase to yourself out loud or in your imagination. For example, awesome, super, cool, I'm good, wow, high, great, excellent, wonderful, perfect... and "action I did".
   - Affirmative head nod
   - Smile
   - You can combine several ways to have a stronger effect. For example, say the phrase "*cool*" in your mind while smiling and head nodding.

2. Before you start playing guitar positively reinforce to yourself that you are learning. For example, a phrase with a smile, "*finally!*"
3. Pick a topic for you to practice and positively reinforce yourself that you chose that topic to practice.
4. When you have completed an exercise or done a small action, *positively reinforce yourself.*
5. When you have finished the exercise - *positively reinforce yourself.*
6. When you start to do the exercise - *positively reinforce yourself.*
7. When you're done playing guitar - *positively reinforce yourself that you played great.*
8. When you've finished the game, think of more moments you did awesome and also *positively reinforce yourself!*

It's also important learning to see small results.
For example - 2 days ago I placed an Am chord within 1 minute. Yesterday I placed an Am chord in 10 seconds. Today I placed an Am chord in 2 seconds.
Or like this. At the beginning of the exercise, I was able to play the fingerpicking 4 times in a row, keeping the rhythm. After 2 minutes of the exercise, I was able to play the fingerpicking rhythm 10 times in a row. And after 5 minutes I was able to play exactly 23 times in a row, and that's very cool, because after 5 minutes I was almost 6 times better than at the beginning of the exercise!

You may not remember positive reinforcement at first when you are learning. This can be solved very easily, print out the positive reinforcement guide and put it next to your guitar so that every time you pick up the guitar you will see a reminder of positive reinforcement.

Give yourself positive reinforcement that you're already studying this book to learn how to play guitar!

PSY.10

How to respond calmly to "mistakes" when playing guitar

When you calmly react to a mistake, the muscles remain relaxed and the attention focus remains on the action you are doing. The brain is trained to keep doing what it was doing in a calm state.

If you scold yourself, say negative comments for a mistake, your muscles will tense up and the physical actions you do will be more difficult and harder. Attention will drift to the negative and the brain will repeat it more often because the unconscious tends to what is in focus.

When I was in high school, I played basketball. And when I was throwing the ball into the hoop, I missed and then I stressed a little bit because I wanted to hit the hoop and I threw the ball past it. In my imagination I mouthed the word "damn". The next time I threw the ball into the ring I kept the memory in my mind of how I missed and tensed up. I threw the ball again, missed and tensed up again because I wanted to hit the ring but missed. And so 5 times in a row I threw and I stressed all the time before I threw, because I kept in my head the memory of the miss and the stress and each time I also said the word "damn". The whole time I was throwing the ball, the coach was watching me. The coach came to me and said in order to accurately throw the ball into the ring, the whole body should be relaxed, while the muscles involved in throwing the ball should be tensed as much as necessary to throw the ball into the ring. If I tense additionally other muscles of the body and tense the muscles that move the arm more than necessary, the trajectory of the ball will change. That's why you need to throw the ball relaxed. The coach said that with each new throw I was stressed more and more, and the ball flew farther away from the target each time. When I completely relaxed and concentrated on the throw, I hit the target easily for the next 10 throws.

That's why it's important to focus on the right action and keep the rhythm.

That's when I first thought about the fact that you should react neutrally to mistakes and just keep doing what you were doing, keeping the rhythm consistent.

So if you want to make more mistakes, you can stress and think about mistakes. But if you want to learn faster, reach your goal with a thrill, then concentrate on the actions you need to do.

Instruction:
1. If you make a mistake, just keep doing what you were doing.
2. Pay attention to your body. If you feel stress in your muscles, relax them.
3. Focus your attention on the task and the action you need to do.
4. Keep doing the actions you need to do.

Let's concentrate on what needs to be done!

PSY.11

How to ALWAYS be in a cool, positive and energetic state of mind when playing guitar. ANCHORS

- Have you ever been walking down the street, thinking about something of your own, and suddenly you see a friend/girlfriend with whom you used to have a great time and your state of mind changes to a positive one?
- Or when you look at photos/videos of a vacation you went on and your state of mind immediately changes to what it was at the moment of taking the photos?
- Or for example, you wake up, look out the window and see that it's raining outside, and your state of mind immediately changes, for example, to depressive, sad. Or vice versa, you see bright sunshine, blue sky and your mood immediately changes to positive.
- Or when you play your favorite song, does your mood change immediately.

Sound familiar? Why it happens.

Imagine ancient people walking through the forest. They heard wolves howling, and then they were attacked by wolves. One man was eaten, and the other man fought in rage, but he was badly wounded. The one who was wounded was healed. So he's walking through the forest again. He hears the howling of wolves again, and instantly remembers his past experience, that when there was such a howl they were attacked by wolves and he fiercely fought with them. So he instantly goes into a state of rage. In this case, the howling of the wolves was the trigger to switch the state to rage.

Our brain remembers every moment in time across all perceptual systems. Taste, smell, pictures, sounds, feelings (state). The brain needs this to learn and understand how to behave in repetitive situations. If one of the triggers is repeated (picture, sound, smell, taste, feeling), the brain switches to the state it had in the past when the same trigger was present.

Have you ever had one of those times when you go to sleep on your bed and can't fall asleep? If so, I'm going to guess, and I'm likely to guess. Not only do you sleep on the bed, but you also watch movies, shows, use your phone, maybe even eat. Am I right? It can be the same with working at a computer, where you often work, watch videos, play games, and eat in the same place. All at the same desk and computer.

The brain gets confused about what to do in this place, whether to go into a relaxed state and fall asleep, or to have fun or to secrete gastric juice to digest food. As a result, the strongest state of all that was in that place is turned on.

That's why it's important to share space. One space = 1 action. On the bed only to sleep, at the computer only to work, in the kitchen only to eat, and so on. If you work at the computer, play games, and eat, I recommend doing the next thing. For example, change your clothes for each activity.

Work at the computer in one piece of clothing, and play computer games in a different color of clothing.

Work on one mouse pad, and play on a different mouse pad (it's important that they are very different).

Work on one chair, play on a different chair (it is important that they are very different).

Make a different user on the computer. One is a work user, with a picture on the desktop, and another user for games with a completely different picture on the desktop.

Then the brain will separate the meanings and you will always be in the right state for each task.

Same with any activity, including **playing guitar**. I highly recommend you have a dedicated space ONLY for playing guitar.

For example:
1. It can be a chair (it is important that it is very different from other chairs in your house in color or shape).
2. A separate room for practicing music (where you do nothing but practice music!).
3. A separate outfit for playing guitar (you only use this outfit for playing guitar).
4. Even the guitar itself will serve as an anchor to transition into the state you play it in! But it is important to play the guitar always in a positive and active state.
5. You can also sit while playing the guitar always to one side. For example, towards the window.

An anchor is a special case of a trigger. It is a stimulus in the real world (or a memory in the imagination) that instantly switches to some state. An anchor can be a specific sound, picture, taste, smell, sensation in the body.

If you already have an inappropriate state of mind in a certain matter, you can change it. For example, if you sit down to work and the state immediately becomes lazy, then to change this state to a productive one, you should ALWAYS enter a productive state before the workspace and immediately sit down to work in this state. After a certain number of such repetitions (1-30) there will be a re-anchoring and the brain will memorize the new state. It is like pouring into a coffee cup one teaspoon of orange juice after another. At some point the cup will run out of coffee and only orange juice.

There are many ways to get into a productive state. I'm going to talk about 2 ways.

METHOD 1. How to enter any state that has been in your life:

1. Say out loud or in imagination "**STOP**".
2. Imagine that all thoughts (pictures that you imagine in your head) break into small pieces and disappear.
3. Take a deep **inhale and exhale.**
4. Ask yourself, what is my task right now?
5. What would be the best state of mind to do this task?
6. Recall a situation in your life where you were in the right state of mind (e.g., **highly concentrated**).
7. Imagine in front of you at a distance of 1 foot yourself in the situation where you were in the desired state. Visualize what your face was like at that time.
8. Move your body to enter into the visualization.
9. Recall in detail everything that happened in that situation according to these parameters:
   • What you saw (consider what was around you and imagine the pictures very vivid, clear, detailed, rich and colorful).

- Listen to the sounds that surrounded you at that time and visualize them louder and closer.
- Remember how you felt in that situation, what were the sensations in your body and intensify these sensations.
- Remember the smells that were there and intensify the smells in your imagination.

This will help you get into the state you want in about 10-50 seconds.

This technique will allow you to get into absolutely any state that you have in your life experience. Whether you feel sad, crying, laughing, happy, angry, energetic, sleepy, alert, concentrated, satiated... Similar techniques are used by actors.

You may find that you can't visualize the images clearly enough. That's okay, do it your way and over time you'll get better and better at visualizing and getting into the state you want.

So, let's play guitar in a separate space and always in a positive and upbeat state!

How to get into a state of aliveness, interest and full concentration. ALPHABET

This is a super exercise that will allow you to get into a very productive state in 5 minutes, warm up your body, synchronize both brain hemispheres and activate the 3 perceptual systems of the brain (visual, auditory and kinesthetic). This exercise is also a great way to train the skill of keeping rhythm, which is VERY IMPORTANT in music! Additionally, this exercise trains the skill of being calm when you make mistakes (any mistakes), which will allow you to learn faster and feel very calm when you make mistakes.

Here are a couple examples of how this exercise helps you improve your results in any area.

I have been trained in the technique of quickly memorizing information and can easily memorize any sequence of numbers. I remember a friend came to my house for a visit and I made a bet with him that while he was writing any sequence of numbers with a pen on paper for 1 minute, I would memorize all those numbers and their sequence while he was writing them. He wrote 54 digits in 1 minute and I barely had time to memorize them because the speed of writing the digits was quite fast. Then I stepped aside and called all the digits and their sequence from memory. Then I remembered the "Alphabet" exercise I had on the wall in my room. I did this exercise for about 5 minutes, entered a very active state and suggested to my friend to do the experiment again, but asked him to write numbers much faster.

He ended up writing 88 digits in 1 minute and I was able to memorize them all with amazing ease! In just 5 minutes of doing the exercise, I increased my memorization performance by 62% by getting into a productive state.

I use the Alphabet exercise every day, even before I pick up my guitar for lessons. It gives me a great state of alertness and high, and in this state I practice the guitar.

METHOD 2. Alphabet exercise

In each rectangular cell there is a letter of the alphabet at the top and a small letter below it, which means which hand should be raised. L for left. R - right. T - together.

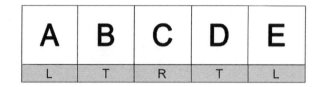

The goal is to choose a calm tempo, roughly like the ticking of a clock hand (1 second).

- Print out the exercise sheet (**QR code on the next page**)
- Hang it on a vertical surface with the center of the sheet at eye level.
1. Stand 4-5 feet in front of the exercise sheet.
2. Recall the interval of the second hand's ticking interval.
3. With your speaking voice as loud as your average conversational voice, say the name of the top letter in the rectangle while simultaneously raising either your left hand if the letter of the alphabet is written l (left) or your right hand if it is written r (right), or both hands together if t is written(t).
4. Keeping an even rhythm, at about the speed of a second hand and with the same volume of voice, reach the last letter in the alphabetical order.

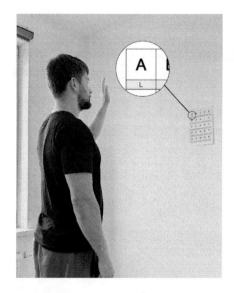

You can do the exercise in any order. A to Z, Z to A. Vertically in a snake-like pattern, horizontally in a snake-like pattern...

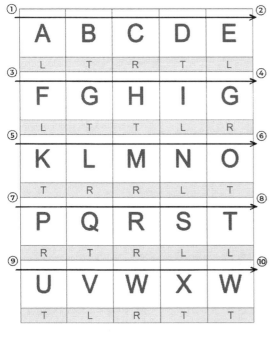 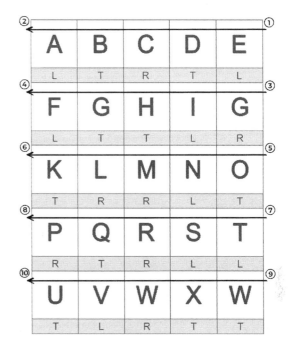

 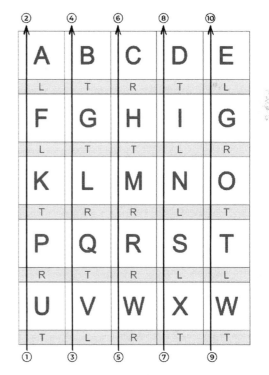

When you get the hang of the exercise, you can do a harder version:
- When you raise your left arm, simultaneously raise your right leg bent at the knee.
- When you raise your right arm, simultaneously raise your left leg bent at the knee.
- When it says "together," stretch both arms out in front of you and do a half squat.

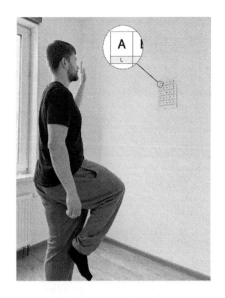
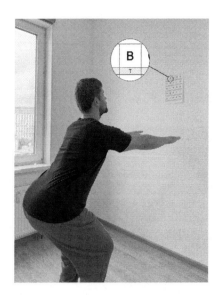

IMPORTANT!

If you made a mistake, just keep doing the exercise in the same rhythm.

If you made a mistake and said a word/phrase out loud (or in your imagination) or stopped doing the exercise, then step aside and jump 5-10 times in the same rhythm you are doing the exercise, saying in a positive state for each jump the phrase "it's fun, it's a game, it's fun, it's a game..." and immediately return to the exercise.

Once you have completed the exercise completely from A to Z without error, track your condition by how much better you feel from 0 to 10 points. If 4-5 points are enough for you, you can start doing things (playing guitar or other things). Or you can do the exercise again and enter the state of productivity on the 10 points level.

It may happen that you don't have a printer. Then you can either print out the exercise from someone you know or from a copy center.

So do the alphabet exercise and see how much better you feel!))

how to do
the alphabet
exercise

Video

Print files

drive.google.com/drive/folders/1Ce4A7nvYsX_jgnRQa_PZ63ElhHt7WHYq?usp=drive_link

Instructions on how to use the QR codes

From a phone:
1. Turn on the QR code reader application on your phone (camera, browser or other application).
2. Point your camera at the QR code.
3. Click on the link.

To download the files:
- Click on the desired file (it should open)
- Click the download icon (Depending on the operating system, the picture may be different)

From a computer:
1. Take a photo of the QR code and send this photo to your computer (to messenger, email or any other way).
2. Download the photo to your computer.
3. In your browser, type "decode QR code online".
4. Open any appropriate site and upload the picture with QR code.
5. The site should transform the QR code into a link. Open the link.

To download the files:
- Right-click on the desired file
- Click download and choose where you want to save the file.

CHAPTER 1
PREPARING TO PLAY THE GUITAR

1.1

How to store a guitar

If you store your guitar properly, it will last for decades and will be in good condition. Its sound qualities will improve because the wood will gradually dry out and the sound will resonate better.

If you store your guitar near a radiator or open window, the wood can become damp, swell and warp. This will cause all the string-holding mechanisms to become loose and the guitar will be permanently detuned.

- **What is prohibited:**

If stored near a radiator, the wood will warp and the guitar will be ruined.

If there are constant temperature or humidity changes in the room, the wood will constantly absorb moisture and warp, causing the guitar to break.

If you store it in a case, the wood will absorb moisture and warp because there is no air exchange in the case.

- **How to store:**

In a room with consistent air temperature. Medium humidity. If it's just a room, you can hang it on a wall hook or put it on a stand away from the window.

So let's store the guitar on a stand or on a wall hook, away from the window.

1.2

Guitar clip-on tuner

Guitar tuning is a must and with the clothespin tuner tuning is very easy. The clip-on tuner can be always put on the top of the guitar and due to this the tuning of the guitar can be done very quickly.

If you tune your guitar in other ways, it will take more time to tune. So make sure you get yourself a clip-on tuner for your guitar.

How to choose a guitar size for an adult and how to choose a guitar size for a child

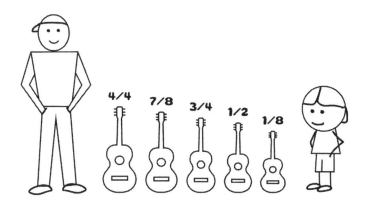

Let's talk about guitar sizes and how to choose a guitar that's the right size for you.

Usually for adults of average height and above, a standard size guitar is suitable. But if you're shorter than average height, or if you're buying a guitar for a child, buying a large size guitar will be painful to play. Hands will be located in other places, not where they should be and because of this muscles will be strained and it will be very hard to play.

I once had a man bring his 10 year old son to my first lesson. They brought their standard size guitar. I told them right away that playing on such a guitar would be a torture for the child. To make it clear, I suggested that the child try to sit down with such a huge guitar. His fingers of his left hand could barely stretch over 2 fret on the neck. Although on a guitar, the fingers should easily stretch over 4-7 fret. His right shoulder was so raised up that he had to strain very hard to reach the strings with his right hand. I suggested going to the store together and picking out a guitar to fit him. At the store we picked up the guitar, the child put his right hand on the top "corner" of the guitar and was easily able to reach the strings in front of the string holder. His left hand fingers easily reached from the 1st to the 4th fret. His father bought this guitar for his son and we were already able to comfortably learn to play the guitar.

How to find the right size guitar

Right hand check:
1. Place the guitar with the lower notch on your right thigh near your belly
2. Place your right hand on the strings in front of the string holder
3. Place your forearm on the top "corner" of the guitar body
4. Make sure that there is at least half a fist's length from where your forearm touches the guitar's edge to your elbow.

Left hand check:
1. Place (without clamping the string) the index finger of your left hand on the 6th string at the 1st fret
2. Place your middle finger on the 6th string at the 2nd fret
3. Place your ring finger on the 6th string at the 3rd fret
4. Place your pinky finger on the 6th string at the 4th fret.

 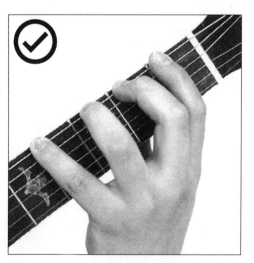

If you are able to put your right hand on the strings and the distance at the point of contact between your forearm and the body of the guitar and your elbow is more than half of your fist and you are able to place the fingers of your left hand from the 1st to the 4th fret on the 6th string, then the guitar is the right size for you. The exact same checking instructions for children. It is best to buy the guitar with your child so they can check that the guitar is exactly the right size for them.

1.4

Footrest

With a footrest, it is more convenient to keep the guitar on your foot and adjust the height of the foot rest. In addition to a special stand, you can use any object that will stand flat on the surface (plank, bottle, massage roller, etc.).

If you play without a footrest, then it is important that the chair is correctly matched in height. We'll talk about chair selection in detail in the instructions on how to sit down with the guitar.

1.5

How to organize guitar lessons

Let's talk about organizing classes. How long is the best time to study and how to study.

If you practice every day, you can learn to play any song in a simplified way (i.e. either with basic strumming or simple strumming) in as little as 1 month. If you practice every day for at least 30 minutes, your brain will memorize new playing skills and you will get better and better each time. Playing every day will develop the small muscles of the hand, which are almost motionless in everyday life, to play the guitar easily and quickly. The muscles in your forearm will become hardy and you'll be able to strum for long periods of time and be comfortable. If you practice every day, you will develop a slight seal on your fingers, which will make you feel comfortable when playing and will give you a ringing sound.

If you play every other day or 1-3 times a week (or a total of less than 3 hours a week), the small muscles in your fingers will fatigue quickly when playing due to lack of regular exercise. The forearm muscles will fatigue clamping the strings for a chord and will be able to play chords for 1-2 minutes and then have to rest. The seals on the fingers will take a long time to form and slowly and because of this the fingertips will be sore longer and the sound will be very quiet when playing. If you play less than 3 hours a week, you will have to spend more time remembering what you practiced. If you play 1-3 times or less than 3 hours a week, you will be able to play songs in 2-3 months instead of a month.

When I started learning guitar I played only 2 times a week for 30 minutes. Every time I remembered where to put my fingers, my hand and forearm muscles got tired in 2-3 minutes. After 5 minutes my back started to hurt. Every new lesson I remembered what chord I practiced last time, remembered where to put my fingers on the strings in that chord... The fingers of my left hand were stiff and it was very hard to play the chord. Also every time after lessons my fingertips were sore because the seals were just starting to form on the first and second day after playing, and on the 3rd or 4th day without stimulation my fingertips became soft again. Then I decided to take the lessons more seriously and started to play regularly for 30 minutes twice a day, i.e. a total of 1 hour each day. At first I paid special attention to sit with a straight back, relaxed neck and shoulders. I set a timer for 30 seconds and when it rang I looked in the mirror opposite me and the mirror to my left, in which I saw my back, neck and shoulders. If I curved my back, I straightened up. I also paid attention in my body to where I was tense and relaxed those areas. This is what allowed me to play for 30 minutes straight and feel relaxed and at ease. After only 7 days, my fingertips had already flattened and my fingers felt comfortable playing.

In the morning after waking up, I sat down to play guitar for 30 minutes.
First I sat down with a straight back, relaxed neck and shoulders. I put the guitar in the right position and then played strumming for 5 minutes with my right hand to play this skill and get my fingers used to playing rhythmically and evenly. Then with my left hand I clamped the strings, for example, the A chord, and with my right hand I played the strings and checked that all the strings sounded. If some strings were muted, I would check the instructions to make sure I had the chord right, and then I would run my fingers over the strings again to make sure I had the chord right. Then I would take my fingers off the strings and put the A chord back on, and so on, practicing different chords (A, Am, Dm, D, D, C, E, Em, G) for 10 minutes. Then I'd start playing right hand fighting on the chords for 10 minutes. That was the end of my morning lesson and I went to do other things. In the evening I would do a second lesson for 30 minutes.
I also sat down with a straight back and relaxed shoulders. I put the guitar in the right position and played strumming for 5 minutes. Then 10 minutes practicing chords with my left hand. Then 5 minutes of playing a fight on a chord. After 5 minutes practicing chord changes. And 5 minutes I played strumming on chords.

After 2 weeks of such regular practice, I was able to play the Sting song Fields of Gold. It was fantastically cool! Then I started to play every day for 2 hours, and on weekends for 3-5 hours and get high from playing the guitar! After such lessons I was able to play Metallica - Nothing Else Matters, Chuck Berry - Johnny B. Goode, Led Zeppelin - Stairway to Heaven and other great songs in a month.

You can of course play only 1-3 times a week and play your first song 2-3 months later. Every time you play you will feel fatigue in your forearm muscles, feel discomfort on your fingertips because they will be soft, but if you want to play your first song after 3-4 weeks, after 5-10 days to feel completely comfortable and instead of feeling "what is this log in my hands", to feel the guitar as a part of your body, to adapt small muscles of the hand and forearm muscles to the game so that they do not hurt and feel comfortable, then read the instruction how to organize your guitar lessons.

Instruction:
1. For the first 2 weeks, check yourself every lesson to make sure that you are sitting straight and relaxed (we will discuss how to do this in Chapter 2).
2. Each lesson, practice chord progressions, overdubbing, and strumming (when you've covered all of these topics).
3. When your left hand gets tired of setting a chord, play overdubbing or warble with your right hand on the open strings to rest.
4. If possible, break up your daily lessons into separate small sessions. For example, 30 minutes in the morning and 30 minutes in the evening. Or 20 minutes in the morning, 20 minutes in the afternoon, and 20 minutes in the evening. Or 30 minutes in the morning, 30 minutes in the afternoon and 30 minutes in the evening. Or 45 minutes in the morning and 45 minutes in the evening.

It may happen that you can't play the guitar for a day. The solution to this is simple - play 1.5 times more in one day or the next day.

So let's play guitar every day!

1.6

Parts of the guitar

The guitar consists of 2 main elements. Body and Neck.

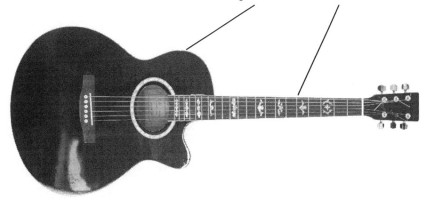

Neck

At the end of the neck there is a headstock, on which tuning pegs are located for tuning the strings.

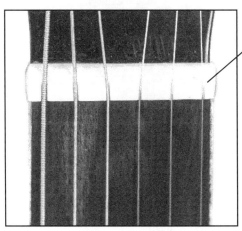

There is a Nut, which has 6 recesses, each of which contains a string.

There are fret markers on the neck to help you navigate better. There may not be any marks.

For example, they are not on a classical guitar. Usually fret markers are placed on the 3rd - 5th - 7th - 9th - 12th frets. For the first acquaintance, it is enough for us to focus on 3 - 5 - 7 frets.

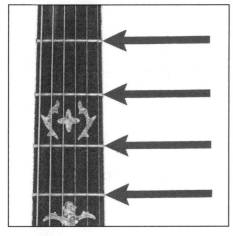

Metal stripes (frets). They divide the string into different lengths and due to this, different notes (sounds) sound.

Body

It is inside the body that the sound becomes so loud and strong due to the resonation inside.

Bridge, on which the strings are attached.

1.7

Guitar string tuning

Let's talk about why it's important to tune your guitar and how to do it correctly.

If you tune your guitar every day before you play, you will develop a correct tuneful ear and a precise pattern of intervals between sounds. If you play a tuned guitar, you will be able to accurately distinguish musical intervals and pick up music by ear. When you master vocals, if you have always played a tuned guitar, you will be able to hit the notes more easily and accurately with your voice. If the guitar is tuned, when you play it, the sound will be nice and beautiful.

The strings on the guitar are tuned differently each time and when you play, your brain will always memorize different ratios between the sounds produced and as a result, your tuneful ear will be poor due to the lack of a precise pattern of intervals between sounds. If the guitar is detuned, you will not be able to pick up the music by ear, because the music will have precise intervals, and the detuned guitar will be a mess of dissonances. Besides, each string is tuned to a specific frequency and if your guitar is out of tune, the sound will be disgusting.

But most importantly, beginners may not be able to hear that the guitar is out of tune because they don't have a tuneful ear yet.

There are 2 ways to tune a guitar.

METHOD 1: Tune your guitar using sound frequency analysis

An application for your phone, computer, or an online program that shows the frequency of the sound in numbers is suitable.

What this method is for.

1. For tuning your guitar when you changed the strings.
2. If the guitar is out of tune by more than 10% of the desired note frequency of each string.

If you don't have a tuneful ear yet, this method will help you tune your guitar very accurately because you'll be guided by precise numbers.

I remember a student came to my first lesson. He took out his guitar, sat down and started trying to play something. I made a surprised face at the strange sound of the guitar and asked him if he could hear that the guitar sounded strange. He said it seemed to sound normal.

I asked him exactly how he tuned the guitar, to which he said he tuned it with a clip-on tuner.

I said he should have tuned each string by frequency first, and then tuned it with a clip-on tuner.

He asked me - "why do you need to tune the guitar by frequency? There is a tuner, it is normal to tune with it".

I said it's fine to tune with a tuner, but the tuner shows the name of the note, not the frequency. For example, the note A comes in 110 Hz, 220 Hz, 440 Hz and other frequencies. And the tuner shows only the name of the note A. But since a beginner doesn't have musical hearing yet, he probably won't realize by ear that the guitar sounds different.

I turned on the clip-on tuner and checked the tuning of his guitar. As I thought, he had tuned the 5th string to note A. It should be, but only the 5th string should be tuned to note A at 110 Hz, and he had stretched it so much that it was tuned to note A at 220 Hz. So he pulled the string twice as hard and didn't even realize it.

I said that if he had tuned the strings by frequency in Hz, he would have tuned the guitar exactly as it should be.

I told him, "Look, I'll show you how to tune the guitar by frequency. Take your phone and type in the internet search term "guitar tuning online with frequency analysis". In the search box, open a site with a sound frequency analysis program. Turn on microphone access. Put the phone next to the guitar. Pull the 6th string and see what the app shows." The app showed 90 Hz. I said to loosen the string tension to 82.41 Hz. Twist the pick to reduce the string tension. He's loosened the 6th string tension to 82.41 Hz. Now pull the 5th string. The program showed 220 Hz. I said the 5th string should be 110 Hz, so you need to loosen the string to 110 Hz. He started twisting the 5th string peg to loosen the tension to 110 Hz.

"Now pull the 4th string." The program read 144.2 Hz.

"Tension the string to 146.83 Hz. Now pull the 3rd string." The program reads 194 Hz. "Pull the string to 196 Hz."

"Now pull the 2nd string." The program reads 241.5 Hz.

"Pull the string to 246.94 Hz."

"Now pull the 1st string." The program reads 331.44 Hz.

"Loosen the string to 329.63 Hz.

I said, "Cool, in my opinion you're doing great because you've done the tuning of the guitar by frequency! Now you need to retune each string again, because when you change the tension of one string the tension of all the strings changes."

He pulled the 6th string and the program showed 81.7 Hz. I said, remember you tuned that string to 82.41 Hz, and now it's 81.7 Hz after tuning all the strings. That's because the overall tension of the strings has changed. We need to retune all the strings again. Eventually he tuned each string again and his guitar started to sound melodic and beautiful. The whole tuning took only 2 minutes.

If you don't care about playing a distressed guitar with a nasty sound and forming a false tuneful ear, you can skip guitar tuning. But if you want your guitar to sound beautiful and you want to develop your tuneful ear so that you can easily pick up songs by ear, then read the instructions for tuning your guitar by frequency.

Instruction:
1. Download an application for your phone/computer to analyze sound frequency. Or find such an application online on the internet. (search for "application that shows sound frequency for guitar tuning" or "guitar tuning online with sound frequency analysis").
2. Allow access to the microphone so that the program can receive the signal for analysis (if online, there is usually a confirmation pop-up on the website).
3. Position the guitar closer to the microphone.

6th string tuning (top string, thickest string) - 82.41 Hz
Pull the 6th string with the finger of your right hand and see what frequency the app shows.
- If the app shows a frequency lower than 82.41 Hz, you need to tighten the string more. To do this, twist the peg on headstock that holds the 6th string. Which

way you twist it will depend on the type of guitar. So if anything, twist both ways to see which way the string is stretched. Twist the tuning peg in the direction of tension until the app shows 82.41 Hz.

- If the app shows a frequency higher than 82.41 Hz, you need to loosen the string tension. Turn the tuning peg toward the slack side to loosen the tension until the application shows 82.41 Hz.

5th string tuning - 110.00 Hz

Pull the 5th string with the finger of your right hand and see what frequency the app shows.

- If the app shows a frequency less than 110.00 Hz, you need to tension the string more. Turn the tuning peg toward the tension side until the app shows 110.00 Hz.
- If the app shows a frequency greater than 110.00 Hz, you need to loosen the string tension. Twist the tuning peg toward the slack side to loosen the tension until the app shows 110.00 Hz.

4th string tuning - 146.83 Hz

Pull the 4th string and see what frequency the app shows.

- If the frequency is less than 146.83 Hz, you need to pull the string tighter. Tighten the string until the app shows 146.83 Hz.
- If the app shows a frequency greater than 146.83 Hz, you need to loosen the string tension. Loosen the tension until the app shows 146.83 Hz.

3rd string tuning - 196.00 Hz

Pull the 3rd string.

- If the application shows a frequency less than 196.00 Hz, tension the string to 196.00 Hz.
- If the application shows a frequency greater than 196.00 Hz, loosen the string tension to 196.00 Hz.

2nd string tuning - 246.94 Hz

Pull the 2nd string.

- If the application shows a frequency less than 246.94 Hz, tension the string to 246.94 Hz.
- If the application shows a frequency greater than 246.94 Hz, loosen the string tension to 246.94 Hz.

1st string tuning (bottom string, the thinnest string) - 329.63 Hz

Pull the 1st string.

- If the application shows a frequency less than 329.63 Hz, tension the string to 329.63 Hz.
- If the application shows a frequency greater than 329.63 Hz, loosen the string tension to 329.63 Hz.

CHECK ALL THE STRINGS AGAIN.

Since the strings and the body of the guitar are a single system, each element affects the whole system. When the tension of one string changes, the guitar neck changes its bend and the load on the other strings is also redistributed, causing the other strings to change their tension. The more the tension of a string changes, the more the tension of other strings changes. Therefore, after tuning each string, you should repeat the entire string tuning procedure until each string is tuned to the correct frequency. When changing strings, this procedure will need to be done 3-7 times because the new strings are very elastic and stretchy. If the guitar has already been tuned and is a little bit out of tune, it is usually enough to tune all the strings 1 time.

So, go to the app that shows the pitch and tune all the strings as instructed!

METHOD 2: Tune your guitar using a clip-on tuner

Why do you need this method? This is a very quick way to tune your guitar while playing, or to fine-tune your guitar if it's a bit out of tune. This way of tuning is very good when the guitar has already been tuned, it's a bit out of tune and needs to be fine-tuned. Or for example, during a performance, between songs, you can use the clip-on tuner to tune your guitar very quickly, literally in 10-20 seconds.

If you attach the clip-on tuner to the headstock and leave it there, then to tune the guitar you only need to press the power button on the tuner and tune all the strings of the guitar. When you've already tuned the guitar 50 or more times, it will only take 10-20 seconds to tune the guitar with the clip-on tuner.

Instruction:
1. Attach the tuner to the end of headstock
2. Press the power button on the tuner
3. Set the tuner mode to "Guitar" (usually just the letter **G**)
4. If the tuner has a tuning frequency selection function, if it is not 440 Hz, set the tuning frequency to **440 Hz**.

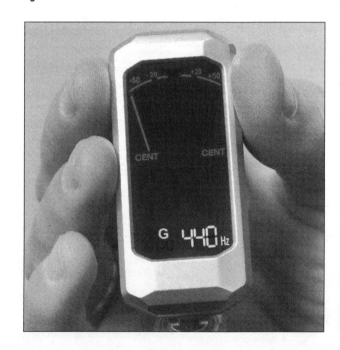

General tuning principle for each string:

- If the arrow is exactly in the middle, the string is perfectly tuned.
- If thve arrow is left of center (or there is no arrow), then you need to tension the string by turning the peg until the arrow is in the middle.
- If the arrow is to the right of the center, you must loosen the string tension by rotating the tuning peg until the arrow is in the middle.

6th string
Pull the 6th string and see what the tuner shows.

- If the tuner shows **6E**, follow the "General Tuning Principle for Each String" instructions.
- If the tuner shows 4D, you must tension the string until the tuner shows 6E and then follow the "General Tuning Principle for Each String" instructions.
- If the tuner shows 3G, loosen the string tension until the tuner shows 6E and then follow the "General Tuning Principle for Each String" instructions.

5th string
Pull the 5th string and see what the tuner shows.

- If the tuner shows **5A**, follow the "General Tuning Principle for Each String" instructions.
- If the tuner shows 3G, you must tension the string until the tuner shows 5A and then follow the "General Tuning Principle for Each String" instructions.
- If the tuner shows 2B, loosen the string tension until the tuner shows 5A and then follow the "General Tuning Principle for Each String" instructions.

4th string
Pull the 4th string and see what the tuner shows.

- If the tuner shows **4D**, follow the "General Tuning Principle for Each String" instructions.
- If the tuner shows 2B, pull the string until the tuner shows 4D and then follow the "General Tuning Principle for Each String" instructions.
- If the tuner shows 1E, loosen the string tension until the tuner shows 4D and then follow the "General Tuning Principle for Each String" instructions.

3rd string

Pull the 3rd string and see what the tuner shows.

- If the tuner shows **3G**, follow the instructions in "General Principle for Tuning Each String".
- If the tuner shows 1E, tension the string until the tuner shows 3G, and then follow the "General Principle for Tuning Each String" instructions.
- If the tuner shows 5A, loosen the string tension until the tuner shows 3G, and then follow the "General Principle for Tuning Each String" instructions.

2nd string

Pull the 2nd string and see what the tuner shows.

- If the tuner shows **2B**, follow the "General Tuning Principle for Each String" instructions.
- If the tuner shows 5A, pull the string until the tuner shows 2B and then follow the "General Tuning Principle for Each String" instructions.
- If the tuner shows 4D, loosen the string tension until the tuner shows 2B and then follow the "General Tuning Principle for Each String" instructions.

1st string

Pull the 1st string and see what the tuner shows.

- If the tuner shows **1E**, follow the "General Tuning Principle for Each String" instructions.
- If the tuner shows 4D, you must tension the string until the tuner shows 1E and then follow the "General Tuning Principle for Each String" instructions.
- If the tuner shows 3G, loosen the string tension until the tuner shows 1E and then follow the "General Tuning Principle for Each String" instructions.

It may happen that the tuner does not turn on. This can be solved by checking the battery, it may need to be replaced with a new one.

So do a guitar tuning with a clip-on tuner!

CHAPTER 2
2.1. GUITAR SITTING

2.1.A-1

How to choose a chair for playing guitar

Let's talk about what kind of chair you should have so you can properly position your guitar on your leg.

If you sit on a chair with the right height, you will be able to put guitar on your foot so that it stands on its own in one place and you can play comfortably. Your right hand will rest relaxed on the guitar and your left hand will hang relaxed on the neck of the guitar. Your right shoulder will be relaxed and you'll be comfortable playing.

If the height of the chair is too high, the guitar will move off your foot and you will have to strain your muscles to hold it. This will cause fatigue and you will have to move the guitar back periodically. If the chair is too low, the angle in the leg bend can be large and then the guitar will rest on the leg too high and you will have to strain the muscles of the right shoulder when playing. This will cause these muscles to fatigue quickly. Because of the muscle tension, your neck vessels will be constricted and this can lead to headaches. If the chair has armrests, your arms will be caught on them and you will have to strain your shoulders to raise your arms higher in order to play. Muscle tension will lead to fatigue.

When beginners come to me for their first class, I start by selecting the right height chair.

Once two brothers of different ages came to my class. One was 16 years old and the other was 11. I asked the older brother to sit on a standard chair, press his buttocks and lower back against the back of the chair. I asked him to put his shins perpendicular to the floor. The guy was very tall, about 6'4" with long legs, and he got a bend angle in his right leg of about 45 degrees. I put the guitar on his foot and asked him to put his right hand on the body of the guitar. I asked him, "are you comfortable sitting like that with the guitar?" He replied that he wasn't.

If he played the way he was sitting now, his back and right shoulder would get tired very quickly because the angle of the bend in his knee is too small (45 degrees), so the guitar stands up high on his hip. Due to this, you have to physically lift your right shoulder up when placing your right hand. The right shoulder is higher than the left shoulder and the back is curved. The muscles on the left side of the body are tense and the muscles on the right side are relaxed, so fatigue will set in quickly. I asked the guy to move to the chair that was higher. He sat down, put his right and left shins perpendicular to the floor and the angle in the bend of his leg was 80 degrees. This is the optimal angle for playing the guitar. We measured the height of the chair and I told him to play on a chair of the same height at home.

The other brother was short, about 5 feet tall, and when I asked him to sit on a standard chair with his buttocks and lower back against the back of the chair, shins perpendicular to the floor, he had a knee angle of about 110 degrees, meaning his knee was well below the top of his thigh. I put the guitar on his right foot and asked him to put his hands on the guitar. The guitar started to move down his leg. I told him that if he played on a chair with that height, he would have to keep his arm muscles tight all the time to hold the guitar, then he would get tired of playing quickly. I brought in a footrest and made a height on the stand so that the bending angle in his right foot became 90 degrees. I gave him this stand so that when he plays guitar at home he can use this stand.

You can sit on any chair, but then the angle in the bend of the leg may be less than necessary and the guitar will move off the leg. You'll have to hold it up and adjust it constantly. Or the angle may be more than necessary, then the guitar will stand too high and you will have to make the right shoulder higher than the left one when you put your right hand on the guitar, which will lead to tension in the right shoulder and fatigue when playing. But if you want your shoulder muscles to be relaxed when playing the guitar, then check your chair as instructed.

Instruction:

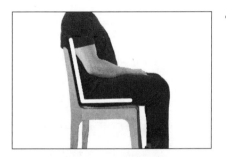

1. Sit on a chair, press your buttocks, lower back and thoracic spine against the back of the chair (or sit on a stool).

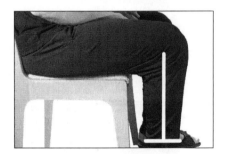

2. Place your shins perpendicular to the floor.

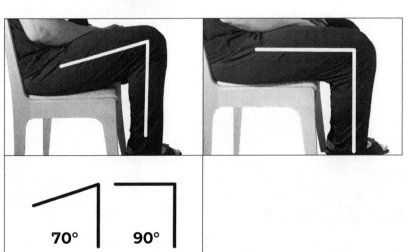

3. Check the angle in the bend of your right leg. If the angle is between 70 and 90 degrees, you're fine.

70°   90°

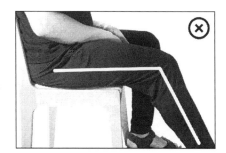

4. If the angle is more than 90 degrees, put something under the leg to make the angle 70-90 degrees.

5. If the angle is less than 70 degrees, get a higher chair so that the bend of your leg is 70 to 90 degrees.

So, sit on the chair, and check the angle of your right leg bend...

2.1.A-2

How to sit on a guitar playing chair

Let's talk about why it's important to sit with a straight back and what happens if you have a hunched back.

When you sit with a straight back, the small intervertebral muscles are toned and the back feels comfortable. With a straight back and correct guitar positioning, the neck stays straight and then the neck feels comfortable and relaxed.

If you hunch your back and sit in this position for 5-10 minutes or more, the small intervertebral muscles will be severely overstretched. If you sit like this every day, the small muscles will become inflamed and increase in volume due to inflammation. Because of the increased volume, these muscles can hit nerve roots. Then back pain will start and sitting will be difficult, the back muscles will quickly become tired and sore. If the back is hunched, there will be a lot of tension in the neck at the place of the curve and the neck will start to ache. If you play with a crooked back on a regular basis, you may get headaches due to the arteries in your neck being constricted.

Once at a master class a guy asked me a question - what to do if your back hurts when playing guitar. I asked the guy at what point his back starts to hurt? He said that after playing the guitar for 10 minutes. I asked him to pick up the guitar and play any song he wanted. He walked over to me, sat down in a chair, picked up the guitar, hunched his back, craned his neck down and started playing. I waited until he finished playing the song and asked him to pay attention to the sensation in his back. He said it was tense. I asked him to straighten his back at the lower back and relax his back muscles to the point where he could sit in the same position. I also asked him to straighten his neck and play the song again with a straight back and neck. He played the song one more time and I asked him how he felt in his back. He said it felt much easier now. Then I suggested that every time he played the guitar he should sit down with a straight back and always pay attention to whether his back was straight and if he hunched it, straighten it again. After 3 weeks he wrote me an email saying that now when he plays guitar his back is relaxed and he feels very comfortable playing!

You can sit with a crooked back, then headaches, neck and back pain can occur. But if you want to feel comfortable and play the guitar for pleasure, read the instructions.

Instruction:
1. Sit on a chair
2. Straighten your back in the lumbar and thoracic spine
3. Relax your back muscles to the point where your back remains straight and in a natural position
4. Straighten your neck and look forward in front of you.

So let's sit with a straight back and neck when playing the guitar.

2.1.A-3

How to hold your shoulders when playing guitar

Let's talk about why it's important to keep your shoulders and upper and middle shoulder blade muscles relaxed.

When your shoulders are relaxed you can play 1-2 hours straight on the guitar and feel lightness in your shoulders and neck. You will enjoy playing and be able to concentrate fully on the learning process.

If you tense the muscles of the middle and top of the shoulder blades, lifting the shoulders during the game and keep them tense, you will get tired very quickly, literally in 5-8 minutes of play. And if you play like this for 20-30 minutes, the tension in your muscles will cause the vessels in your neck to constrict and you may get a headache.

One day on a guitar forum website I saw this post:
"I started playing guitar, but I can't understand, every time I play my neck and shoulders start hurting a lot. I can't understand why."
In response, I wrote back to tell him to pay attention to the feelings in his shoulders, upper and mid shoulder blade muscles when practicing guitar. That after 1 minute of playing, he should pay attention to whether those muscles are relaxed or if there is micro-tension? One minute later pay attention to whether these muscles are relaxed or whether there is micro-tension? After another minute, I paid attention again... And so every minute.
I wrote to him that I assumed he was gradually tensing the muscles in his shoulders and shoulder blades and only noticed the tension when it was already very strong. So I suggested that 5 times a minute I move my attention to my body and feel if my shoulders and shoulder blades are relaxed. If they are not relaxed, then relax them. Then a man wrote back that he tried doing as I say and immediately noticed that as soon as he sat down to play, he started to tense his muscles a little bit. He started relaxing them right away and keeping track that if there was a micro-tension, he relaxed them right away. He said he played guitar for an hour straight. For the first 15 minutes he was constantly tracking tension and relaxing, and then he just became comfortable playing and after an hour he felt fine.

You may not be able to keep track of whether your shoulder muscles are relaxed or not. You may tense them up and get tired quickly, but if you want to be relaxed and enjoy playing the guitar, then read the instruction manual.

Instruction:
1. Sit in a chair with a straight back and neck
2. Bring your arms down, relax your shoulders
3. Notice the sensation at the top of your shoulder blades, relax this part as much as possible
4. Notice the sensation in the middle part of your shoulder blades, relax this part as much as possible
5. In your imagination, count from 1 to 5
6. Repeat from point 3 - 10 times.

So let's relax the shoulder and upper shoulder blade muscles when playing guitar.

2.1.A-4

Placing the guitar on the foot

Let's talk about how to place the guitar on your foot to make it comfortable to play and what happens if you place the guitar any other way.

If you put the guitar in the correct position, the neck will be straight and the neck muscles will be relaxed. The back will be straight and the muscles of the spine will be almost relaxed. When the guitar is set up correctly, it will be very easy to put the right hand in the correct position and it will be very comfortable to play. The fingers of the right hand will automatically take a 45 degree angle to the strings and plucking the strings will be very easy. The right shoulder muscles will be relaxed. The shoulder part of the left arm will be almost in a vertical position, due to this the biceps of the arm will be relaxed, which will allow you to play easily and comfortably for more than 1 hour in a row. It will be comfortable to strum chords with the left hand and the strings will sound tuneful.

If you put the guitar on your foot in the wrong way, your neck muscles will tense up, causing the blood vessels in your neck to become constricted and blood to the brain to flow poorly. This can cause a headache. Also with tense neck muscles due to lack of blood supply to the brain there will be a sleepy state while playing the guitar. If you put the guitar far away from your stomach, your spine will curve forward, your back muscles will be tense and after 5-8 minutes your back muscles will be tired. The right hand will not be resting on the guitar, but will be held overhanging by the muscles, because of this the shoulder muscles will be tense and tire quickly. The fingers of the right hand will be scraping on the strings and making a nasty sound. If the guitar is placed on the foot as it is, the biceps of the left arm will strain and fatigue. When you strum chords with your left hand, your fingers and palm will hit the strings and muffle them.

I was approached by a student who has been playing guitar for 6 months now. He said that his main problem is that his neck hurts and every day or every other day in the evening he has a headache. He has to take painkillers. When he sits down to play the guitar after about 15 minutes, his back muscles are already very sore, his right shoulder is tense and he has to take a rest after 15-20 minutes of playing the guitar.

I asked him to demonstrate how he plays and as soon as he picked up the guitar everything became clear to me. He put the guitar on his right leg almost at the knee, his guitar was parallel to the horizon. He leaned his body forward, his right shoulder up and his right hand on the body of the guitar. His neck was hunched down to look at the strings on the fingerboard. It goes without saying that muscles get tired very quickly in this position!

I asked him, " Do you want some magic?" He was surprised and said yes.

I asked him, " Can you get a guitar stand and put the guitar next to you at arm's length so that when you sit down you can pick up the guitar from the stand?"

He says, "I can."

I said, "Put it down." He put the guitar next to him. "Sit on the chair. Take the guitar and place it with the lower neck on the middle of your right thigh. With your left hand, grasp the guitar's fingerboard at the first fret, and with your right hand, grasp the body of the guitar on the right side."

I asked, "Can you sit with a straight back and neck?"

He said, "I can."

I said, "Sit with a straight back and neck.

Make the length of the guitar parallel to the horizon line.

Can you keep the guitar parallel to the horizon line and move the guitar down your leg until the bottom of the guitar rests on your stomach? "

He said, "I can."

I said, "Move it." He moved the guitar down his leg until it touched his stomach.

"Remember geometry?"

"Remember what?"

I said, "Angles. Do you remember what a 30-degree angle looks like?"

"Of course I remember."

I said, "With your left hand, hold the guitar fingerboard 30 degrees away from you."

Then with your right hand, tilt the top of the guitar body towards your chest until you can see the 1st lower string.

He's like, "Okay, got it."

I said, "Great. Now with your left hand, raise the head of the guitar up to the height of 1.5 of your fists. Next, place the forearm of your right hand on top of the guitar body and relax your right hand. And now place the thumb of your left hand on top of the first fret of the fingerboard. Relax your left hand so it's just hanging on your thumb.

He said, "Done."

I said, "Congratulations, you've mastered proper guitar placement. Now your neck and sapina will be relaxed when playing the guitar." The only thing left to do now is to put the left and right hands correctly.

Then I explained to him how to put the left and right hands correctly and after the guy played like that for 6 days he called me and said that he has been doing well for 6 days, his neck is relaxed, his back is relaxed, he plays 30-40 minutes calmly. If before he had a headache every day or every other day in the evening and drank painkillers, he has been feeling great for 6 days now!

Of course you can put the guitar as you like, and then you may have back pain, neck muscles, headache because of the tension of the muscles of the neck and right shoulder, but if you want to play the guitar with a high, to be relaxed and full of energy, then we go to the instructions on how to put the guitar.

Instruction:
1. Put/stand the guitar next to you at arm's length so that you can pick it up from a sitting position.
2. Sit on a chair (a chair that you have correctly "How to choose a chair for playing guitar" - **page 37**).
3. Take the guitar in your hands.

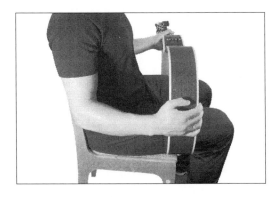

4. Place the guitar with the lower notch on your right foot in the middle of your thigh.

5. With your left hand, grasp the guitar's fingerboard around the 1st fret. With your right hand, grasp the body of the guitar with your right hand.
6. Straighten your back and neck (face parallel to the vertical).
7. Straighten the guitar so that its length is parallel to the horizon line.

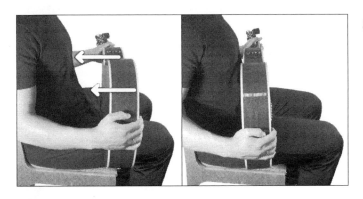

8. Keeping the guitar parallel to the horizon line, move the guitar along your leg toward your abdomen until the bottom of the guitar body rests against your pubic bone, or the bottom of your abdomen if your abdomen protrudes beyond the pubic bone.

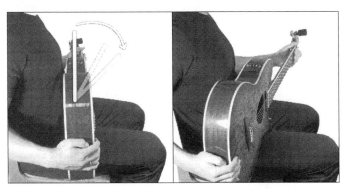

9. With your left hand, move the head of the guitar away from you in a 30-45 degree horizontal plane.

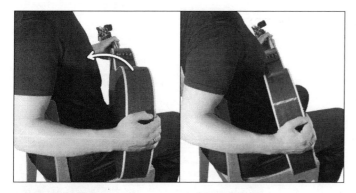

10. Sitting with a straight back and neck, tilt the top of the guitar body toward your chest until you can see the first string.

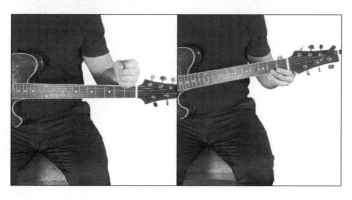

11. With your left hand, raise the head of the guitar up to the height of 1 of your fists.

12. Place the forearm of your right hand on top of the guitar body and relax your right hand.

13. Place the thumb of your left hand on top of the fingerboard head near the first fret and relax your hand so that it hangs only on the thumb. It is important that all the muscles of the hand are relaxed (it just hangs on the thumb).

So, perform the guitar placement as instructed 10 times in a row to feel and memorize the correct guitar position.

2.1.B

How to position your right hand for playing the guitar

If you set your right hand correctly, you will easily be able to perform various playing techniques such as strumming or fingerpicking. You will also be able to play fingerpicking very easily. And most importantly, you will feel comfortable playing because the shoulder and forearm muscles of your right hand will be relaxed!

If you put your right hand in any way, your forearm muscles will get tired very quickly and you will play for a maximum of 7-10 minutes at a time. And your right shoulder muscles will also get tired and it will be hard to play. If you learn to play crooked with your right hand, with years of practice it can lead to tunnel syndrome.

Tunnel syndrome is severe pain in the joint of the hand due to the twisted position of the hand when playing the guitar. Therefore, it is very important to do everything correctly and according to the instructions!

Back in the 90's when I first started learning to play guitar, I learned to play from videos on cassette tapes. At that time I didn't understand why I could only play for about 10 minutes, and then my right forearm and hand joint started to hurt a lot. At some point I came across a guitar video school where the teacher talked about the importance of positioning your right hand correctly at the very beginning of your learning. I started comparing my playing to the way the teacher showed me on the video and I finally realized! I was holding my right arm in the air, straining my shoulder and I was also bending my hand sideways, which made my forearm muscles tired.

I repeated all the steps that were in the video.

First, I sat in the basic staging position with the guitar on my foot. Then I gathered the fingers of my right hand into a fist. I turned my right hand palm to palm and at the bottom of my palm on the left side I felt a rounded bone protruding. This bone I placed it 1/4 inch behind the 5th string behind the bridge, and with my bent fingers I touched the strings. Then I imagined that the guitar was inscribed in a rectangle and placed my right forearm where the corner of the guitar was. When I put my forearm down I felt the support on the guitar and relaxed my right shoulder muscles because my forearm was just resting on the guitar.

Then I straightened my thumb and put the left side of the thumb tip pad on the 5th string. I put the middle of the index finger tip pad on the 4th string. I put the middle of the pad of the tip of my middle finger on the 3rd string. I put the middle of the pad of the tip of my ring finger on the 2nd string. I put the middle of the pad of the tip of my little finger on the 1st string.

I checked the angle between my forearm and the strings and it was about 30 degrees. Then I started raising the head of the guitar higher with my left hand, until the angle between my right forearm and the strings was 45 degrees. Then I lifted my fingers off the strings, leaving the bottom bone of my palm lying behind the 5th string behind the bridge, and with my left hand I ran my fingers over the strings on the neck to check that all the strings were sounding. The 4th and 5th strings were muted. I moved the bone of my right hand further behind the bridge by 0.25 inches and again ran my left hand over the neck strings. The 4th and 5th strings were still muted. I moved the left bone 0.25 inches behind the bridge again, ran my left hand over the strings and now all the strings were sounding. The video recommended practicing the whole setup 5 times, but I did it even cooler. I did right hand placement 20 times in a row, then I closed my eyes and started visualizing in detail as if I were standing behind me and looking at myself doing the right hand placement in every detail as instructed. I imagined this scene 5 times in a row and each time this imaginary movie was faster and faster. Then I picked up the guitar and immediately put my right hand in the right position in one motion! I played in that position for 30 minutes and surprisingly I felt great!

I know more than 10 of my students who have played with a side-bent hand for a long time, got tunnel syndrome and periodically suffer from pain in the hand. So it's up to you to follow my instructions to make it easy and comfortable for you to play or not to follow the instructions.

Instructions - how to place the right hand in fingerpicking position.

1. Sit on a chair with a straight back and place the guitar on your foot following the instructions for placing the guitar on the foot (**page 41**).
2. Gather the fingers of your right hand into a fist, leaving the fingers relaxed.

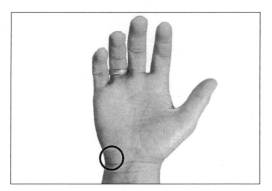

3. Turn your right hand with the palm facing you and feel the lower bone on the left side, which protrudes from the bottom of your palm.

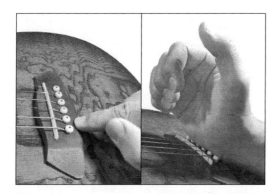

4. Place this bone behind the 5th string behind the bridge of the guitar about 1/4" away.

Later, when you play fingerpicking (2.2. Exercises 1-15), try putting the bone not behind the 5th string, but between the 5th and 6th. And also try putting it behind the 6th string. Depending on the size of your hand, you may find one of these positions comfortable. Pay attention to which position you feel more comfortable playing, and play in that position.

5. Keeping your fingers bent, touch the strings with them.

6. Imagine that the body of the guitar is inscribed in the shape of a rectangle.

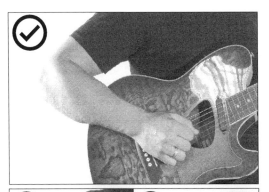

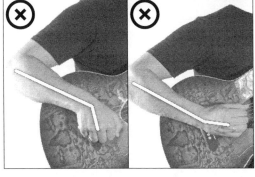

7. Place your right forearm on the imaginary corner of the rectangle. Make sure that the forearm and hand are in a naturally flat position, i.e. the imaginary axis of the forearm and the axis of the hand are on the same line.

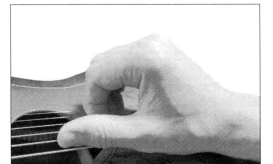

8. Extend the fingers of the right hand and:
   a. Straighten your thumb completely. Place the left side of the pad of the tip of your thumb on the 5th string.
   b. Place the middle of the tip pad of your index finger on the 4th string.
   c. Put the middle of the pad of the tip of your middle finger on the 3rd string.
   d. Put the middle pad of the tip of the ring finger on the 2nd string.
   e. Place the middle of the tip pad of your pinky finger on the 1st string.

9. Check the angle of your forearm to the strings. If it is less than 45 degrees, raise the head of the guitar higher with your left hand until the angle between the strings and your forearm is 45 degrees (+/- 5 degrees).

Instruction. Checking the correct positioning of the right hand for fingerpicking the strings

1. Raise the fingers of your right hand 1 inch above the strings, leaving the bone of your lower palm lying where you put it (behind the 5th string behind the bridge).

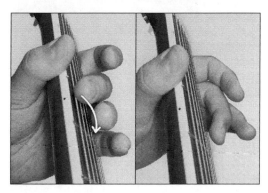

2. With the middle finger of your left hand, swipe the strings on the fingerboard:
    *   If there is no muffled sound and all strings are sounding, all is well.
    *   If any strings are muffled, move the palm bone of your right hand 0.25 inches further behind the bridge and check again from step 9 until all strings are sounding.

Right now practice your right hand positioning using these instructions at least 10 times! The purpose of this exercise is to teach you to put your hand in the correct position right away.

When you have practiced the right hand position more than 10 times, do the following practices:

PRACTICE 1. Guitar foot placement and right hand placement
After you've practiced your right hand placement, let's combine picking up the guitar and right hand placement into a single movement.
1. Follow all the steps in the instructions for putting the guitar on your leg
2. Follow all the steps in the right hand positioning instructions
3. Lay the guitar away from you
4. Repeat all steps from the beginning

Practice the united movement **10 times** in a row to solidify this fundamental skill!

PRACTICE 2. Guitar foot placement and right hand placement in imagination
Do all the same steps as in the previous practice, only now in imagination.
With eyes open or closed:
1. Imagine yourself (like you're looking at another person) doing the entire guitar foot placement and right hand placement in detail as instructed. Scroll through the imaginary movie 3 times.
2. Imagine in first person (like you're looking out of your own eyes) as you do the entire guitar foot placement and right hand placement in detail as instructed. Play the imaginary movie 3 times.

This exercise is needed to reinforce the skill pattern of landing, guitar foot placement, and right hand placement.

2.2. RIGHT-HANDED PLAYING. STRINGS FINGERPICKING

2.2.A

Right-handed playing

The role of the right hand in guitar playing is rhythm and stroke. I would say that the right hand is the leading hand in guitar playing. The left hand just clamps the right places on the strings, changing sound pitch, and the right hand creates the sound and creates the rhythm!

There are 2 main types of right-handed playing.
Playing with your fingers and playing with a flatpick (picking).
In classical guitar education, you learn to play with your fingers first. I am also an advocate of learning to learn to play with the fingers first and here's why:
Almost all healthy adults have well-developed fine motor skills in their fingers. This is especially true for right-handed playing because most people are right-handed. When a beginner puts the fingers of his right hand on the strings he can at least somehow pluck them, because he knows how to control his fingers. Each finger plucks only one string and it's very comfortable. Fingers are a part of our body and we can easily feel where we need to move our finger to get to the right place.
If a beginner picks up a flatpick, there are a lot of nuances. First of all, for a beginner the flatpick is a foreign object and the brain will miss the strings when controlling the hand. Also, the flatpick must be held correctly and you will have to develop the skill of holding the flatpick, which is an additional 5-10 clean hours of habituation. The flatpick should be placed at a certain angle to the strings and constantly held at this angle. To play with a flatpick you need to relax your hand at the moment of swinging and tense it at the moment of striking. The movement of the flatpick involves both the hand and the forearm, it is a complex coordination movement. When fingerpicking, it is very difficult to hit the strings with the flatpick. Even experienced guitarists need more control when fingerpicking with a flatpick. Playing with a flatpick often involves the technique of muting the strings, so you need to learn to control your hand so that you can mut strum some strings and keep others open. A flatpick can be dropped while playing and if you only play with a flatpick, you will have to interrupt your playing to pick up a flatpick and if you play in front of an audience, stopping your playing will look terrible. But if you're playing with your fingers you'll be fine, or if you know how to play with your fingers and a flatpick, then if you lose the flatpick you'll be able to continue playing with your fingers.

Playing with a flatpick is a very cool way of right-handed playing, and it opens up new playing possibilities. So be sure to learn the flatpick in the future when you have basic guitar skills. We will be exploring flatpick playing in book 3 of the guitar instruction book series.

Action	Fingers	Flatpick
Motor skills are developed	+	-
Basic muscle coordination	+	-
Ability to play immediately	+	-
Lack of forearm control	+	-
Easy control of movement	+	-
Always with you	+	- (you may drop)

There are 2 main types of finger play:
1. Fingerpicking
2. Strumming

2.2.B

How to play fingerpicking

When you master fingerpicking with the correct technique, the sound will be nice and even. It will be comfortable to play. You will be able to play beautiful lyrical ballads and play chords beautifully. For example, the beginning of Metallica's song Nothing Else Matters is played by fingerpicking the strings. If you play a song by Timbaland, OneRepublic - Apologize on the guitar, it will be played by fingerpicking the strings. The verse of Bob Dylan - Like a Rolling Stone is fingerpicking on the guitar. Led Zeppelin - Stairway To Heaven is played by fingerpicking the strings. If you play Leonard Cohen - Hallelujah on the guitar, it is best played by fingerpicking.

If you suddenly decide to put your fingers as it turns out, then you can face the fact that your fingernails will hit the strings and make a clacking nasty sound. Or if you hang your fingertips deep under the strings, it will be hard to play and the sound will be rhythmically jagged. If you skip learning to play with your fingers, you lose about 50% of all the songs in the world that are played fingerpicking. And maybe even more than 50%, because you can play a mixed style of Fingerpicking and Strumming in the same song.

I remember when a girl came to my lesson with a problem that she was very bad at fingerpicking. I asked her to play fingerpicking. She sat down in the basic position with a straight back and neck, made the correct guitar foot placement, put her right hand on the body of the guitar. She placed her thumb on the 5th string so that the flesh of the fingertip went strongly under the string, about halfway up the upper phalange. The same with her index finger, middle finger and ring finger, she also put them on the strings so that half of the phalange of the finger went under the string. She started plucking the strings and expectedly, she got a clanking sound and a crooked, jagged rhythm when plucking. I told her to stop and suggested she make adjustments to her finger placement.

The first thing I suggested was to see how far she put her fingertips under the strings, as much as halfway up the upper phalanges of her fingers. This is more than should be normal by a factor of 2-3 times! I suggested that she put her fingers on the strings with the middle of the tip of the fingertip. In this case, the fingertip only goes under the string about 1/10th of an inch. She placed the mids of the tips of her index, middle and ring finger pads on the strings and tried plucking the strings. Afterward she yelled out, "Wow, this is so much easier to play!"

The second thing I suggested doing was to pay attention to how she plucked the string. I asked her to pluck the 4th string with her index finger and notice that the moment her finger plucks the string the movement ends with the nail. That is, the plucking of the string starts with the soft part of the fingertip and the plucking itself ends with the nail. That's what made it make a clanking sound like a "whoosh". I suggested that when plucking, she take her finger off the string until her finger slides the nail across the string. She started plucking the string and removed her finger when the soft part of her finger was still on the string. It made a nice tinkling sound. She played like that with each finger separately for 2 minutes and she ended up with a nice, beautiful sound.

You can pull the strings any way you want, but then you can get a clacking sound and it can be difficult to play, because your fingers are too deep on the strings. But if you want to play comfortably and have a nice sound, read the instructions.

Instructions. How to play fingerpicking with the thumb, index and middle fingers of the right hand.

1. Sit in a basic position with the guitar on your foot and do a right hand placement.
2. Pull the 5th string with your thumb and listen to the sound. If the nail touches the string, then:
   - Check the length of your nails. If they protrude beyond the tip of your finger, they need to be trimmed to the bare minimum, while still being comfortable for your fingers.
   - While plucking the string, you slide from the pad of your finger to the nail and finish the motion with the nail plate. Then just start removing your finger a little earlier while the string is still on the soft part of the fingertip.

Do the check in step 2 for each finger. Pull the 4th string with your index finger and check step 2. Pull the 3rd string with your middle finger and check step 2. Pull the 2nd string with your ring finger and check. Pull the 1st string with your little finger and check at step 2.

3. When plucking the string, the thumb stays almost straight and moves towards the index finger 1/3 to 1 inch. You can try plucking the string and resting your thumb on your index finger. Try it both ways and pick a more comfortable way for yourself.
4. The index, middle, ring and pinky fingers bend inward about 1/3 to 1 inch into the palm of your hand when plucking.
5. When you go back, each finger wraps around the string in an arc-shaped path so that the string continues to sound until you put your finger on the string again to pluck.

So let's play fingerpicking now!

2.2.B - Video

Finger trajectory when plucking and pulling back.

2.2. Exercise 1

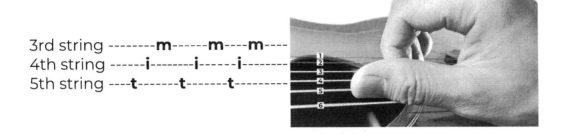

Visualizing this exercise as a picture, it would look like this:

```
3rd string --------m------m----m----
4th string ------i--------i------i--------
5th string ----t------t------t--------
```

Where: **t** - thumb, **i** - index finger, **m** - middle finger.

The 5th string is at the bottom, because when you sit with the guitar, and if you look at the neck, the 5th string will be closer to you, i.e. at the bottom relative to your vision, and the 3rd string will be higher relative to your vision.

Sit up straight and place your right hand in the basic fingerpicking position.

You can leave your ring finger and pinky finger on the 1st and 2nd strings, or take them off the strings and keep them relaxed. With your left hand you can grab the beginning of the neck, put it on your foot or rest it wherever you like. Now we will play only with the right hand.

Maintaining equal time intervals between plucking the strings:

1. Pluck the 5th string with your thumb
2. Pluck the 4th string with your index finger
3. Pluck the 3rd string with your middle finger
4. Do it all over again (loop the movement)

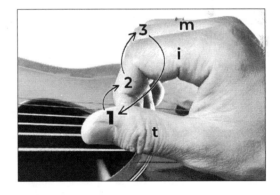

The purpose of the exercise is to give you the initial experience of plucking strings, to feel the movement of the fingers of the right hand, and to practice the looping (circular) movement of the fingers from the thumb to the ring finger.

Play this fingerpicking for 2-3 minutes. After that, if necessary, take a break for a few minutes and start exercise 2.

If you don't feel comfortable with your hand, try rotating your hand a little on the axis toward you.

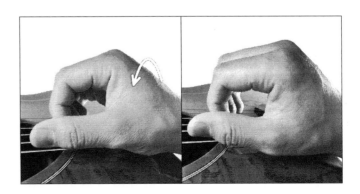

2.2. Ex.1

2.2. Exercise 2

Now play the same thing starting from the 4th string. To do this, move the bottom bone of the palm of your right hand, which you put behind the 5th string, down to the level of the 4th string. And further, when you will play fingerpicking not from the 4th, but from the 3rd string, also shift the lower palm bone down behind the 3rd string. This way, when fingerpicking on other strings, we just shift the whole position down or up, depending on where you play!

Put your thumb on the 4th string, index finger on the 3rd string, middle finger on the 2nd string.

Maintaining equal time intervals between plucking the strings:

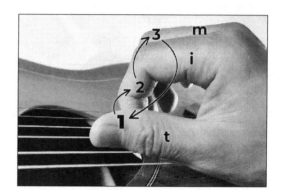

1. Pluck the 4th string with your thumb
2. Pluck the 3rd string with your index finger
3. Pluck the 2nd string with your middle finger
4. Do it all over again (loop the movement)

t - thumb, **i** - index finger, **m** - middle finger.

```
2nd string --------m------m----m----
3rd string ------i--------i------i--------
4th string ----t-------t------t---------
```

The purpose of the exercise is to give you experience playing other strings and to feel the movement of shifting the position of the right hand when playing fingerpicking.

Play this fingerpicking for 2-3 minutes.

2.2. Ex.2

Now play fingerpicking starting on the 3rd string. To do this, shift the entire hand position downward by placing the bottom palm bone behind the 3rd string.

Maintaining equal time intervals between plucking the strings:

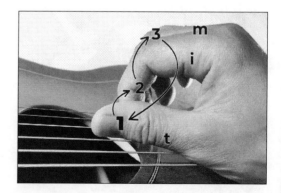

1. Pluck the 3rd string with your thumb
2. Pluck the 2nd string with your index finger
3. Pluck the 1st string with your middle finger
4. Do it all over again (loop the movement)

```
1st string --------m------m----m-----
2nd string -----i--------i------i--------
3rd string ----t-------t------t---------
```

2.2. Ex.3

Play this fingerpicking for 2 or 3 minutes.

P.S. Notice if there is tension in your shoulders, neck or back? If so, check to see if your back is straight? Is your neck straight? Are your shoulders relaxed?

2.2.C

Checking body position and guitar placement when playing

You've already started playing the first exercises and now it's time to talk about tracking the correct body position when playing.

If you check yourself whether you are sitting with your back straight, whether your neck is straight, whether your shoulders are relaxed, whether your left and right shoulders are parallel to the horizon line, your further learning will be comfortable. This skill will become automatic and your muscles will always be relaxed and you will feel good during and after playing the guitar.

If you skip the check and sit with your back crooked, your neck down, your shoulders slumped, your muscles will start to ache and instead of enjoying playing, you will be tired. Because of the constriction of blood vessels in the neck by tense muscles, you may get a headache and be lethargic.

When I first started learning to play, I played guitar about 2 days a week. When I would sit down with the guitar, I would feel tension in my back and neck after a few minutes. But then I would chalk it up to that and just kept playing tense. I ended up getting tired quickly.

When I decided to seriously learn guitar and started playing every day, one of the important things was to always be relaxed when playing guitar. That's when I came up with a cool method. I bought 2 mirrors each about 3 feet tall and wide, put one mirror in front of me and the other one on the side to my left so that when I played guitar, I was able to look in the left mirror and see what my back looked like from the side. And was able to look in the mirror in front of me to see if my shoulders were down and parallel to the horizon line. During the playing of the game, I would set a timer that went off every 30 seconds. When the timer went off I froze in the position I was sitting and looked in the mirror in front of me. If I saw that one shoulder was lower than the other, I relaxed my shoulders and aligned them with the horizon line. Then I looked in the left mirror and saw what condition my back was in. If I had a humped back, I straightened my back, if I had a drooping neck, I lifted it. After that, I quickly paid attention in my body to how I was feeling. Do I have any tension? And if I felt any tension, I relaxed that area. Then I'd play for an hour every day. When I paid 2 times attention to the way I was sitting on a timer every minute, then for 1 hour of playing I did 60*2=120 body position checks and 120 times relaxed the not relaxed places in my body. I played like this for 2 weeks, which is 14 net hours of play. During these 14 hours of play I (120*14) 1680 times checked my sitting position and 1680 times relaxed my body. After that I had already built up a habit of automatism and without a timer I quickly paid attention to my body, how I felt, what position my body was in and corrected myself instantly. It was so automatic that I didn't even notice myself relaxing and correcting my body.

You can just sit as you sit, forget about checking your body position and tolerate muscle tension. Then you'll get tired of the game quickly. But if you want to feel relaxed while playing and feel light after playing, then read the instructions.

Instruction:

1. Take/buy 2 mirrors each measuring more than 3 feet wide and high.
2. Place the 1st mirror in front of you +/- your height so that you can see your upper body in it.
3. Place the 2nd mirror to your left +/- your height so that you can see your upper body from the side.
4. Set a timer for 30 seconds. (an app that makes one or few beeps every 30 seconds works well).
5. When the timer goes off:
   a. Freeze in the position you are sitting.
   b. Look in the left mirror. If your back is hunched, straighten it. If your neck is slumped, raise it.
   c. Then look in the front mirror. If any shoulder is up, relax the shoulder so that your shoulders are relaxed and in line with the horizon.
6. After checking yourself in the mirrors, switch your attention to the feeling of the body. Feel if there is tension somewhere and if there is, relax those places.

You may find it inconvenient to check yourself every 30 seconds. Then you can set a timer for 1 minute or 2 minutes.

So let's set the timer and check your body position during the game, correct your body and relax your muscles!

2.2. Exercise 4

Move your right hand into the position of playing from the 5th string. To do this, place the bottom bone of your palm behind the 5th string, place your thumb on the 5th string, your index finger on the 4th string, and your middle finger on the 3rd string. This exercise is very similar to the previous ones, only one difference is the movement. Now the movement goes in the opposite direction, from the middle finger to the thumb.

Maintaining equal time intervals between plucking the strings:

1. Pluck the 3rd string with your middle finger
2. Pluck the 4th string with your index finger
3. Pluck the 5th string with your thumb
4. Do it all over again (loop the movement)

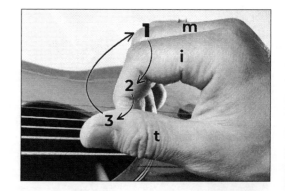

```
3rd string -m-------m-------m-------
4th string ----i---------i---------i-----
5th string --------t-------t--------t---
```

Play this fingerpicking for 2 or 3 minutes.

2.2. Ex.4

2.2. Exercise 5

Same thing, but play 2nd, 3rd, 4th strings.
Move the position of the hand and fingers to the 4th,3rd,2nd strings.

Maintaining equal time intervals between plucking the strings:

1. Pluck the 2nd string with your middle finger
2. Pluck the 3rd string with your index finger
3. Pluck the 4th string with your thumb
4. Do it all over again (loop the movement)

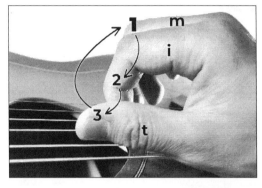

```
2nd string -m-------m-------m-------
3rd string  -----i---------i---------i-----
4th string  --------t--------t--------t---
```

Play this fingerpicking for 2 or 3 minutes.

2.2. Ex.5

2.2. Exercise 6

Same thing, but play 1st, 2nd, 3rd strings.
Move the position of the hand and fingers to the 3rd, 2nd, 1st strings

Maintaining equal time intervals between plucking the strings:

1. Pluck the 1st string with your middle finger
2. Pluck the 2nd string with your index finger
3. Pluck the 3rd string with your thumb
4. Do it all over again (loop the movement)

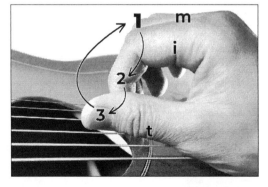

```
1st string ----m-------m------m-------
2nd string  -----i---------i--------i-----
3rd string  --------t-------t-------t---
```

Play this fingerpicking for 2 or 3 minutes.

2.2. Ex.6

2.2. Exercise 7

Now let's play the same exercise, but fingerpicking backwards. **t - i - m - i**.

Move your hand position to the 5th string and place your thumb on the 5th string, index on the 4th string, and middle on the 3rd string.

Maintaining equal time intervals between plucking the strings:

1. Pluck the 5th string with your thumb
2. Pluck the 4th string with your index finger
3. Pluck the 3rd string with your middle finger
4. Pluck the 4th string with your index finger
5. Do it all over again (loop the movement)

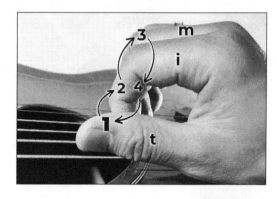

```
3rd string -----m-------m-------m------
4th string ---i----i---i-----i---i-----i----
5th string --t--------t--------t-----------
```

Play this fingerpicking for 2 or 3 minutes.

2.2. Ex.7

 2.2. Exercise 8

Same as the previous one, just move the stance and fingers to the 4th-3rd-2nd strings.

```
2nd string -----m-------m-------m------
3rd string ---i----i---i-----i---i-----i----
4th string --t--------t--------t-----------
```

2.2. Ex.8

Play this fingerpicking for 2 or 3 minutes.

 2.2. Exercise 9

Same as the previous one, just move the stance and fingers to the 3rd, 2nd, 1st strings.

```
1st string ------m-------m-------m------
2nd string ---i----i---i-----i---i-----i----
3rd string --t--------t--------t-----------
```

2.2. Ex.9

Play this fingerpicking for 2 or 3 minutes.

FINGERPICKING EXERCISES WITH FOUR FINGERS (t - i - m - r)

2.2. Exercise 10

Now let's play fingerpicking with 4 fingers of the right hand. Let's add the ring finger to the movement. You can leave your little finger either on 1 string, or take it off the strings and hold it as you like.

Put your thumb on the 5th string, index finger on the 4th string, middle finger on the 3rd string, ring finger on the 2nd string.

Finger movements **t** - **i** - **m** - **r**.

t - thumb, i - index finger, m - middle finger, r - ring finger.

Maintaining equal time intervals between plucking the strings:

1. Pluck the 5th string with your thumb
2. Pluck the 4th string with your index finger
3. Pluck the 3rd string with your middle finger
4. Pluck the 2nd string with your ring finger
5. Do it all over again (loop the movement)

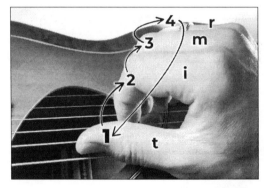

```
2nd string ----------r--------r--------r------
3rd string  ------m------m------m-------
4th string  ----i--------i--------i-----------
5th string  --t--------t--------t------------
```

The purpose of the exercise is to improve your fingerpicking skill, and to practice fingerpicking with 4 fingers.

Play this fingerpicking for 2-3 minutes.

2.2. Ex.10

2.2. Exercise 11

Now shift the entire hand position one string lower. Thumb on the 4th, index finger on the 3rd, middle finger on the 2nd, ring finger on the 1st. And play the same fingerpicking as in the last exercise, but from the 4th string.

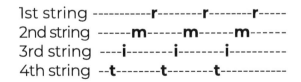

```
1st string ----------r--------r--------r-----
2nd string  ------m------m------m------
3rd string  ----i--------i--------i----------
4th string  --t--------t--------t------------
```

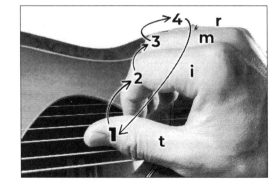

Play this fingerpicking for 2-3 minutes.

2.2. Ex.11

2.2. Exercise 12

Now play the movement from the ring finger to the thumb. Put your thumb on the 5th, index finger on the 4th, middle finger on the 3rd, ring finger on the 2nd.
Finger movements **r** - **m** - **i** - **t**.

Maintaining equal time intervals between plucking the strings:

1. Pluck the 2nd string with your ring finger
2. Pluck the 3rd string with your middle finger
3. Pluck the 4th string with your index finger
4. Pluck the 5th string with your thumb
5. Do it all over again (loop the movement)

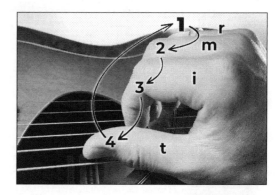

```
2nd string --r--------r--------r------------
3rd string  ----m------m------m----------
4th string  -------i--------i--------i-------
5th string  ---------t-------t-------t-----
```

Play this fingerpicking for 2-3 minutes.

2.2. Ex.12

2.2. Exercise 13

Same as the previous one, just from the 4th string.

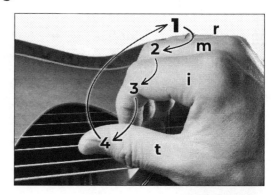

```
1st string ----r--------r--------r------------
2nd string  ----m------m------m----------
3rd string  -------i--------i--------i-------
4th string  ---------t-------t-------t-----
```

Play this fingerpicking for 2-3 minutes.

2.2. Ex.13

2.2. Exercise 14

Now let's play fingerpicking with 4 fingers with circular movement. The movement goes like this: **t - i - m - r - m - i**

Maintaining equal time intervals between plucking the strings:

1. Pluck the 5th string with your thumb
2. Pluck the 4th string with your index finger
3. Pluck the 3rd string with your middle finger
4. Pluck the 2nd string with your ring finger
5. Pluck the 3rd string with your middle finger
6. Pluck the 4th string with your index finger
7. Do it all over again (loop the movement)

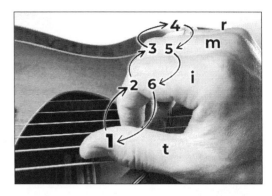

```
2nd string ---------r-------------r------------
3rd string ------m--m------m--m--------
4th string ----i---------i---i---------i-------
5th string --t------------t------------------
```

Play this fingerpicking for 2-3 minutes.

2.2. Ex.14

2.2. Exercise 15

Same as the previous one, just from the 4th string.

2.2. Ex.15

```
1st string ----------r-------------r-----------
2nd string ------m--m------m--m--------
3rd string ----i---------i---i---------i------
4th string --t------------t------------------
```

Play this fingerpicking for 2-3 minutes.

Your task is to work out these fingerpicking so that the sound is without sudden jerks, is even in rhythm and even in dynamics (so that there is no such thing that one fingerpicking is very quiet and the other fingerpicking is very loud), the sound should be approximately the same volume. This can take anywhere from 30 minutes to several days of training. Everyone will have a different learning speed and that's okay.

The speed of learning depends on the amount of indirect experience you already have (finger motor skills, sense of rhythm, and other skills).

Watch a video example of a poorly practiced play and a well practiced play.

Once you've mastered fingerpicking, move on to the next topic. There, we'll start learning left-handed chord progressions, and once you've mastered left-handed chord progressions, we'll combine fingerpicking on the chord!

2.3. CHORDS

2.3.A

What should be the length of the nails on the left hand to play chords

If your nails are the right length, you'll be able to clamp the strings easily.
If the length of the nails is too long, the nails will get in the way of clamping the strings, or will rest on the guitar neck, damaging the guitar and the nail itself.

Yesterday (at the time of writing this text) I sat down to play the guitar and when I put a chord I felt that my nails are resting on the guitar neck, with the ring finger barely clamping the string and because of this the string rattles.

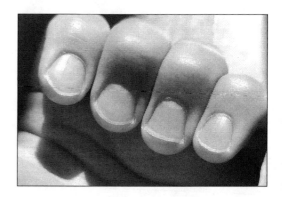

Here are my nails, which I consider to be long and it's not good for me to play with these nails.

I went to get some nail clippers. Since I already know how long my nails need to be, I cut them as I go, but if I didn't know, I would do the following.
I would put the tip of my index finger on the 4th string at the 4th fret perpendicular to the string and press it down. Next, I would check to see if the nail is resting on the neck pad or not. If it does, and the string is rattling or muffled, I would trim the nail to such a length that there would be a gap between the fingerboard and the nail at least the thickness of 2 sheets of paper. I would do the same with the rest of my fingers, also placed perpendicular to the string and check the length of the nails.

You can leave the nails as they are, but if they are too long, your nails will rest against neck overlay and it will be either very hard or impossible to place the chord. But if you want the chord to be comfortable, check the length of your nails.

Nail length check:
1. Place the tip of the index finger of your left hand on the 4th string at the 4th fret perpendicular to the string and press it down. If your nail rests on the neck pad and the string is not pressed down, you should make your nail shorter so that there is a distance between the pad and the nail at least the thickness of 2 sheets of paper.
2. Perform the check in step 1 for the middle finger, ring finger and little finger.

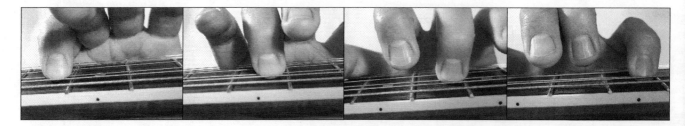

It may happen that your finger is anatomically such that the nail is already very short, but still rests on the overlay. Then play as is or put your finger pads on the string with the place that is farther away from the nail.

So check the length of your nails and trim them if necessary.

Guitar chords

If you learn how to play chords, you will be able to play a lot of songs, because all music is based on chords and their alternation. If you get the chords right, you will be able to quickly memorize which fingers should be pressed in which chord. You'll be able to place the chord and the strings will sound good.

If you play the chord the way you do, the strings will be muffled, your fingers will hit the neighboring strings, and the sound will be terrible.

How to read guitar chord diagrams using the Am chord as an example

In this book, we learn classical chords. All fingers except the thumb are used in their placement.

You and I have already learned how to sit on a chair and put the guitar on your foot, how to put your right hand and how to play fingerpicking. Now we've started learning classical chord placement, and how to use the thumb in piano-type chord placement is what you and I will be learning in Book 2 of the Guitar Learning Series.

Let's number the fingers of your left hand. To do this, turn your left palm toward your face and look at it.

The index finger will be - 1. Middle finger - 2. The ring finger - 3. Little finger - 4.

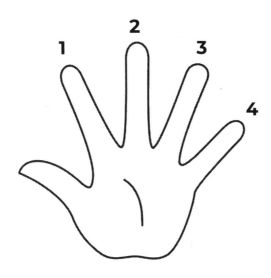

Lay the guitar neck on the left side of the guitar, back on your thighs, strings facing up, and look left at the guitar neck at the zero fret. The **Am** chord will look like this.

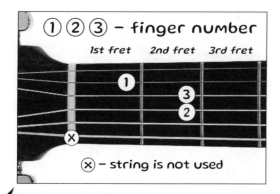

The numbers on the diagram are the number of the finger that clamps the string. Look, the number on the diagram is located on a specific string and on a specific fret. Where "**x**" is drawn, that string is not used in the chord. Where nothing is drawn, it means that the string does not need to be clamped, it just stays open.

- Look at the 1st string on the chord diagram. Nothing is drawn on it, so the 1st string remains open.
- Look at the 2nd string on the chord diagram. The number is located on the 1st fret. The number 1 represents the index finger. This means to place the tip of your index finger on the 1st fret of the 2nd string.
- Look at the 3rd string in the chord diagram. The number is located on the 2nd fret. The number 3 represents the ring finger. This means to place the tip of the ring finger on the 2nd fret of the 3rd string.
- Look at the 4th string in the diagram. The number is located on the 2nd fret. The number 2 represents the middle finger. This means to place the tip of the middle finger on the 2nd fret of the 4th string.
- Look at the 5th string in the diagram. Nothing is drawn on it, which means the 5th string is left open.
- Look at the 6th string in the diagram. It has an "x" drawn on it. This means that this string must be muted with your thumb (we'll talk about how to mut the string later).

2.3.D

General principles of chord placement with the left hand

If you follow the general principles of chord placement with your left hand, then:
You will be able to place the fingers of your left hand correctly on the string so that you can grip the string with minimal force, keeping the hand comfortable and the strings sounding good.
You will be able to place your finger so that there is space between the soft part of your finger and the neighboring strings so that the strings can sound.
You will be able to place your palm correctly under the guitar neck so that the 1st string can oscillate and sound safely.

If you skip the principles of chord placement with your left hand, you may find that your fingertips may touch neighboring strings and muffle them. Your index finger may touch the 1st string and muffle it. You'll have to put a lot of pressure on the string because you put your finger in the wrong place.

I was once approached by a man who works as a salesman and learns guitar in his spare time. He was learning to play on his own and had a problem that he was putting a chord, the strings were muted and there was no sound. He says to me, "Well, look, here's the deal. I'm playing this Am chord, and I'm not getting anything. You see, only the 5th string sounds, the other strings are rattling or muffled."

I smiled and said, "It's gonna sound."

"Look at the way you're strumming the 4th string. Your middle finger is very far away from the metal fret strip, so you're having a hard time gripping it and the string is rattling because it's loosely gripped. Put your middle finger in the middle of the 2nd fret." He put his middle finger in the middle of the 2nd fret, plucked the 4th string and it sounded good.

I asked him, "Do you know why you have the 3rd string muted?"

He asked again: "Why?"

I said, "Why don't you check if you're holding the 3rd string with your ring finger?"

He looked at his ring finger, which was barely touching the string. Then he clamped the string with his ring finger and the string began to sound.

"Now check your index finger on the 2nd string. You most likely have a weak pressure on the string." He clamped the 2nd string on the 1st fret and the string began to sound.

"And that leaves the first string. It's muffled because you didn't put your palm forward under the neck, so your index finger is muffling the first string and no matter how you twist your finger, the string will still be muffled".

You need to bring the bottom of your palm forward under the neck so that the first lower bend line of your index finger is under the 1st string and the first lower bend line of your pinky finger protrudes about 1/2 inch under the first string." He corrected his palm and as a consequence, there was space between his index finger and the 1st string, making the 1st string sound!

"Come on, run it over all the strings," I said. He swiped the strings and all the strings sounded good!

He was like, "Wow, that's great. It's so easy! I was worried I couldn't get it right."

I told him, "Now, every time you have a string that's tinkling or muffled, use the checklist I'm going to give you to finger, then all the strings will sound good."

So. You can skip the instructions and try to put the chord yourself, but then you may face the fact that your strings will be muted, and how to make them sound look for ways to do it yourself, spending hours of your time. But if you want to set a chord so that it sounds 1-3 times, then read the instructions.

General principles of chord placement with the left hand:

1. All fingers clamping the strings of a chord should be arc-shaped.

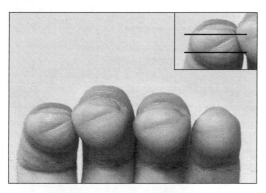

2. Strings are clamped with the middle of the tip of the fingertip, not closer than 1/10 inch to the nail, otherwise you can spoil the nail and not further than 1/10 inch from the center of the tip of the fingertip, otherwise the flesh of the fingertip will touch the adjacent string and muffle it.

3. If you look from above, the strings are always clamped just behind the metal strip. If you clamp in the middle of the fret, you will have to clamp the string harder. If you clamp at the beginning of the fret, the string may rattle. If you clamp the string on the metal strip itself, the pad of your finger will muffle the string and it will sound muffled.

The exception is chords in which the finger positions are under each other, such as the middle and ring fingers in an Am chord. In this case, it is physically impossible to place all fingers right behind the metal strip, and some finger will clamp the string right behind the metal strip, and some finger will be placed in the middle of the fret.

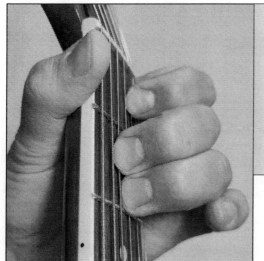

Listen to the difference in sound

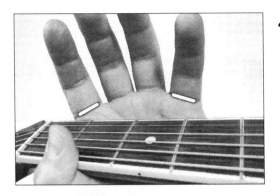

4. From underneath the neck, the palm of the hand should be brought forward so that there is space between the palm and the neck. It is important that the first lower bend line of the index finger is under the 1st string or slightly further away, and the lower bend line of the little finger is 1/3 to 1 inch under the 1st string. This is so that there is space under the index finger so that the 1st string can oscillate freely.

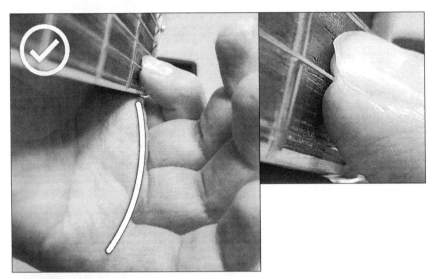

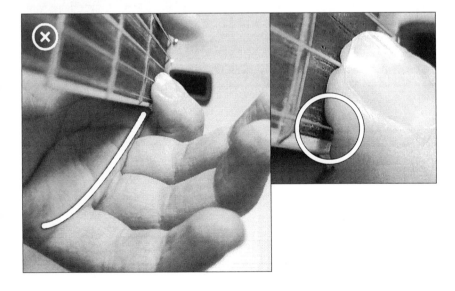

2.3.E

Instruction - how to place fingers in an Am chord

Place the forearm of your right hand on the body of the guitar and relax your hand.

Basic hand position for the Am chord:

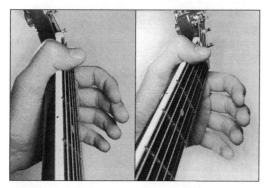

1. Place the thumb pad of your left hand on top of the guitar neck above the metal fret strip of the 1st fret, touching the 6th string. Relax the shoulder muscles of your left hand to use your thumb as a hook on which to hang your hand. If you keep your thumb at the back of the neck, your hand will no longer be able to hang on your thumb and the biceps of your left arm will strain more to keep your arm bent. Because of this, the muscle will tire more quickly, so you need to keep the arm hanging relaxed on the thumb.

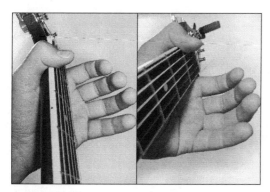

2. Rotate your palm out from under the neck and make sure that the lower bend line of your index finger is under or over the 1st string, and that the lower bend line of your pinky finger extends 1/3 to 1 inch out from under the 1st string so that the 1st string can swing freely under your index finger. Also make sure that there is enough distance between the palm of your hand under your pinky finger and the 1st string to allow the string to swing freely when playing.

Finger placement:

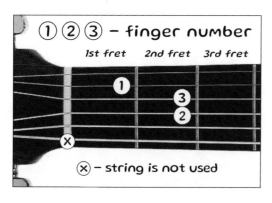

① ② ③ – finger number

1st fret   2nd fret   3rd fret

① ③ ②

ⓧ

ⓧ – string is not used

1. Bend your middle finger and place the center of the tip of the fingertip in the middle of the 2nd fret of the 4th string.
2. Bend your ring finger and place the center of the tip of the fingertip just behind the metal strip on the 2nd fret of the 3rd string.
3. Bend your index finger and place the center of the fingertip just behind the metal strip on the 1st fret of the 2nd string.

4. The pinky finger remains in a relaxed state on the weight.
5. Lift your thumb off the neck, relax it and place it on the neck in the position you are comfortable with. It will get into the position that is comfortable for you. Memorize your thumb position, and next time you play the Am chord, put your thumb in the same place.

Place the **Am** chord and move on to checking if the chord is correct.

2.3.F

Checking the correct placement of the Am chord

Place an **Am** chord. With your right thumb, swipe the strings one by one (from the 6th to the 1st string) to check that all strings are sounding...
If all the strings are sounding, you've done it!

If a string is muffled or rattling, you need to check that string:

Checking the 6th string:
- The 6th string should be muted. If it sounds, you have either not touched it with your thumb or you have pressed it too hard. If you haven't touched it, touch it with your thumb. If it is too tight, release the pressure of your thumb so that it just touches the string.

Checking the 5th string:
- Check to see if the thumb of your left hand is touching the 5th string. If so, move the thumb higher.
- Check if the tip of your middle finger touches the 5th string. If it does, move your middle finger a little lower on the 4th string.

Checking the 4th string:
- If your middle finger presses the 4th string at the end of the fret, press the string in the middle of the fret.
- Check if you have pressed the string hard enough with the tip of your middle finger.

Checking the 3rd string:
- Do you grip the string with the tip of your ring finger, and do you grip it hard enough?
- Check that the place where the string is pressed is just behind the metal strip on the 2nd fret.

Checking the 2nd string:
- Does the pad of your ring finger touch the 2nd string?
- If so, check if you are pressing the string with your fingertip? And is your finger arched?
- Is your index finger pressing the 2nd string just behind the metal strip? If not, press the string just behind the metal strip.
- Is your fingertip pressing the string hard enough?

Checking the 1st string:
- Does the middle of the finger pad touch the 1st string? If it does, check if you have made your finger arched? If yes, but the string doesn't sound, check if the lower bend line of your index finger is under the 1st string? If not, bring it behind the 1st string. Does the lower bend line of your pinky finger protrude 1/3 to 1 inch from under the 1st string? If not, bring it out.
- Check to see if the palm of your hand is touching the 1st string? If yes, bring your palm lower.
- Have you clamped the string with the tip of your index finger pad? If not, clamp the string with the tip of your fingertip.

Be sure to shift your attention to your body and check to see if your shoulders, upper and mid-blades are relaxed? Is your back straight? Are your shoulders straight? Relax your muscles if they are not relaxed.
If you need to, rest for a couple minutes and move on to the next exercise.

2.3. Exercise 1

Memorizing Am chord placement technique

The purpose of this exercise is to give you experience so that you learn to place your fingers simultaneously instead of alternately. If you use your fingers alternately when playing songs, you will hear a lot of false notes and the sound will be terrible. It is necessary to put a chord with all fingers at the same time so that when you change chords you can quickly put the right chord and your playing will be rhythmic and beautiful.

When you have about 100 chord progressions in total, you will be able to play the Am chord with all fingers simultaneously and all the strings of the chord will sound at once!

Instruction:
Let's repeat what you've already done. Basic hand position for the **Am** chord.

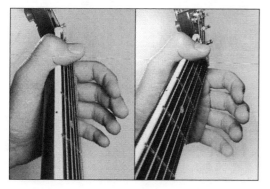

1. Place the pad of your left thumb on top of the guitar neck above the metal fret strip of the 1st fret, touching the 6th string.
Relax the shoulder muscles of your left hand to use your thumb as a hook on which to hang your hand.

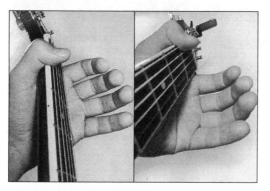

2. Rotate your palm out from under the neck and check that the lower bend line of your index finger is under the 1st string, and the lower bend line of your pinky finger protrudes 1/3 to 1 inch from under the 1st string.

Am Chord

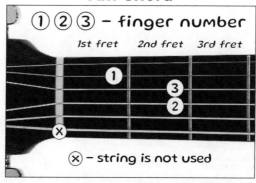

① ② ③ – finger number

1st fret   2nd fret   3rd fret

ⓧ – string is not used

Finger placement for an Am chord

1. Look at the 4th string in the middle of the 2nd fret. Imagine bending your middle finger and placing your fingertip on the 4th string in the middle of the 2nd fret.
2. Look at the 3rd string just behind the metal strip on the 2nd fret. Imagine bending your ring finger and placing your fingertip on the 3rd string just behind the metal strip on the 2nd fret.
3. Look at the 2nd string just behind the metal strip of the 1st fret. Imagine bending your index finger and placing your fingertip on the 2nd string just behind the metal strip of the 1st fret.

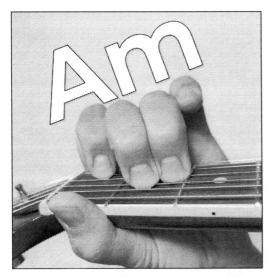

4. Imagine that you have already placed the entire Am chord.
   The tip of the middle finger is on the 4th string in the middle of the 2nd fret. The tip of the ring finger is on the 3rd string just behind the metal strip on the 2nd fret. The tip of the index finger is on the 2nd string just behind the metal strip on the 1st fret.
   Above your fingers imagine a white inscription with black outlines "Am" the size of your fist - *this is necessary to memorize the chord placement, its name and then quickly*

5. In reality, begin to slowly* and simultaneously bend your middle, ring, and index fingers, moving them to the places on the strings where you have already clamped them in your imagination. When you have clamped the strings again, imagine a white inscription with black outlines "Am" the size of your fist and say "**Am**" out loud.
slow fingerings are only for learning. When you learn to finger a chord, you'll finger it fast.

6. Use your right thumb to alternate strumming the strings and check that all the strings of the chord sound. If any string does not sound, check that string - "Checking the correct placement of the Am chord. If all the strings sound, leave your thumb on the neck and bend the other fingers about 80%.
7. Given the basic position of the hand for the Am chord, do it all over again from **step 1**.

P.S. Imagining how you move your fingers, imagining the chord name inscription and saying the chord name out loud is only necessary when you are learning how to place a chord. When you learn how to place a chord, you can just place the chord.

Do this exercise at least 15 times in a row. Rest for a couple of minutes and move on to the next cool exercise!

2.3. Exercise 2

Fingerpicking on an Am chord

In this exercise we combine what we have already learned.
Right-hand fingerpicking + left-hand Am chord placement.

Reread *"Instructions for Right Hand Fingerpicking"* (**page 52**) again to get your right hand in the correct position. And return to this exercise.

- Place your right hand in fingerpicking position from the 5th string (thumb on the 5th string, index finger on the 4th string, middle finger on the 3rd string, ring finger on the 2nd string.
- With your left hand, play an Am chord (so that all strings except the 6th sound).

The movement is as follows: **t - i - m - r - m - i**

Maintaining equal time intervals between plucking the strings:

1. Pluck the 5th string with your thumb
2. Pluck the 4th string with your index finger
3. Pluck the 3rd string with your middle finger
4. Pluck the 2nd string with your ring finger
5. Pluck the 3rd string with your middle finger
6. Pluck the 4th string with your index finger
7. Repeat from **step 1**.

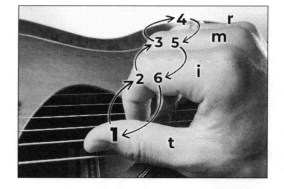

```
2nd string ---------r-------------r-----------
3rd string  ------m--m------m--m--------
4th string  ----i----------i---i----------i------
5th string  --t------------t-----------------
```

2.3. Ex.2

Play 2.3. Exercise 1 and 2.3. Exercise 2 for 1-3 days
(2-5 hours of total playing time).

The criterion for moving on to the next exercises is that you can play the Am chord quickly and simultaneously with all fingers, and all strings sound. You are comfortable playing fingerpicking on the Am chord. Most importantly, you are no longer consciously controlling the chord placement + fingerpicking and you can play it automatically.

The next exercises will build on the previous ones, so if you skip practicing the previous exercises, it will be very hard to master the new ones. If you haven't practiced "2.3. Exercise 1 and 2.3. Exercise 2", then practice them!

Guitar Tablature. How to read guitar tablature

Look at the picture below. This is called guitar tablature.

```
1st string   -----------------------------------
2nd string   --------1-----------1--------------
3rd string   ------2--2--------2---2-----------
4th string   ----2------2----2-------2---------
5th string   -0-----------0--------------------
6th string   -----------------------------------
```

To understand what is drawn on it, let's remove the finger numbers that clamp the Am chord and look at the chord diagram functionally.

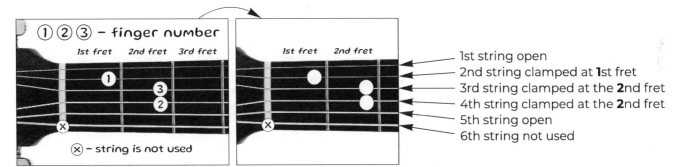

The numbers on the tablature indicate the fret number at which the string should be pressed.

The number 0 means the zero fret, or in simple terms, the open string.

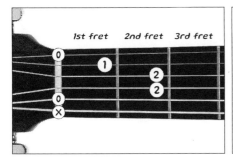
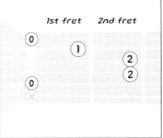

If the chord Am is written in numerals, the result will be.

```
1st string   -0--------------
2nd string   -1--------------
3rd string   -2--------------
4th string   -2--------------
5th string   -0--------------
6th string   ----------------
```

And if you play it fingerpicking, it goes like this.

```
1st string   -----------------------------------
2nd string   --------1-----------1--------------
3rd string   ------2--2--------2---2-----------
4th string   ----2------2----2-------2---------
5th string   -0-----------0--------------------
6th string   -----------------------------------
```

2.3. Exercise 3

This is the same exercise as the previous one (2.3. Exercise 2), where you played fingerpicking on the chord Am, only now we add 1 additional note, thanks to which a musical movement will appear.

Remember that each finger plays its own string? In the current exercise, the thumb plays the 5th string, the index finger plays the 4th string, the middle finger plays the 3rd string, and the ring finger plays the 2nd string.

If you haven't read the previous thread, "**2.3.G.** How to Read Guitar Tablature (on the previous page)", read it to understand what the diagram depicts.

This is a fingerpicking of an Am chord.
In your right hand, you play a circular (looped) motion:
t - i - m - r - m - i

```
1st string     -----------------------------------------------
2nd string   ----------1(r)--------------- 0(r)------------
3rd string   ------2(m)--2(m)-----2(m)--2(m)-------
4th string   ----2(i)--------2(i)--2(i)----------2(i)------
5th string   --0(t)------------0(t)----------------------
6th string   -----------------------------------------------
```

If we remove the abbreviations of fingers from the scheme (we have already realized which finger is used to pluck which string) and leave only numbers, we will get a guitar tablature.

```
1st string     ----------------------------------
2nd string   --------1-----------0-----------
3rd string   ------2--2--------2---2---------
4th string   ----2------2----2-------2-------
5th string   -0-----------0------------------
6th string   ----------------------------------
```

If you look at the figures in the tablature above, you'll see that this string fingerpicking consists of 2 circles.

If we count each plucking aloud, you would need to lift your index finger about 1/3 of an inch between counts 6 and 1. And you would also need to put your index finger back between counts 6 and 1. So in the first round you plucked the 4th string on count 6, and then you lift your index finger about 1/3 of an inch. When you play the 2nd round, between the count of 6 and 1, press the string back with your index finger.

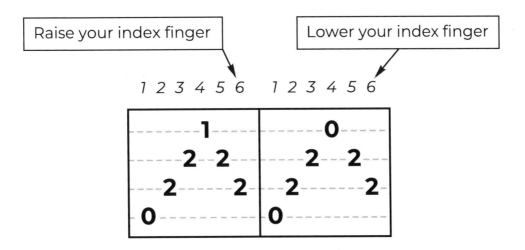

The goal is to loop the movement by keeping equal time intervals between plucking the strings. Play the first circle, raise your index finger about 1/3 of an inch, play the second circle, lower your index finger, and start again from the first circle.

```
1st string   ----------------------------------
2nd string   --------1-----------0-----------
3rd string   ------2--2--------2---2---------
4th string   ----2------2----2-------2-------
5th string   -0----------0-----------------
6th string   ----------------------------------
```

Play this exercise until you feel that you can play it confidently. It may take up to 60 minutes of total playing time for this exercise. In the next exercise we will add one more note, so if you don't master the current exercise and move on to the next one, it will be difficult to play the next exercise.

Interesting fact. The second round of fingerpicking, where you remove your index finger, is the Asus2 chord. Why it's called that, how it came to be, how and where to use it in songs, what kind of artistic effect it has, we'll be discussing with you in the 3rd book of the guitar learning series.

2.3. Ex.3

2.3. Exercise 4

Placing the C Chord

Read "2.3.D. General Principles of Left Hand Chord Progression" (**page 66**) again, and when playing a C chord, make sure that all points of these principles are observed.

Basic hand position for a C chord:
Place your thumb in the same way as in the Am chord.

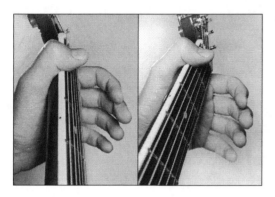

1. Place your thumb in the same way as in the Am chord.

2. With a counterclockwise rotating motion of the hand, place the middle of your palm under the guitar neck and press the place where the thumb starts on the palm of your hand against the guitar neck. Thanks to this, your palm will be strongly moved out from under the neck and lower bend line of your little finger will be much farther out from under the neck than in the Am chord. This is necessary for easy placement of the C chord.

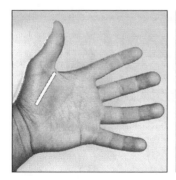 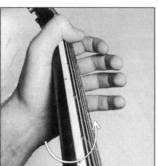 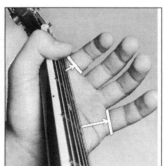 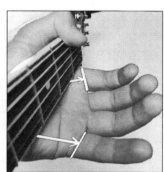

C Chord

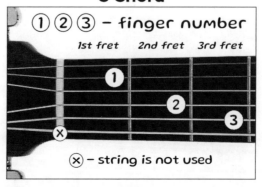

① ② ③ – finger number

1st fret   2nd fret   3rd fret

① ② ③

ⓧ – string is not used

2.3. Ex.4

Finger placement in a C chord:

1. Look at the 5th string just behind the metal strip on the 3rd fret. Imagine bending your ring finger and placing your fingertip on the 5th string just behind the metal strip on the 3rd fret.

2. Look at the 4th string just behind the metal strip of the 2nd fret. Imagine bending your middle finger and placing your fingertip on the 4th string just behind the metal strip of the 2nd fret.

3. Look at the 2nd string just behind the metal strip of the 1st fret. Imagine bending your index finger and placing your fingertip on the 2nd string just behind the metal strip on the 1st fret.

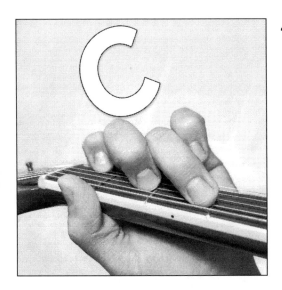

4. Imagine in your mind how you have already placed the entire C chord. The tip of your ring finger is on the 5th string just behind the metal fret of the 3rd fret. The tip of your middle finger is on the 4th string just behind the metal strip on the 2nd fret. The tip of the index finger is on the 2nd string just behind the metal strip of the 1st fret. Above your fingers, visualize a white lettering with black outlines "C" the size of your fist. This is necessary to memorize the chord placement, its name and then quickly remember how this chord is placed.

5. In reality, start slowly* and simultaneously bending your ring finger, middle finger and index finger, moving them to the places of the strings where you have already clamped them in your imagination to set the chord C. When you have clamped the strings again, imagine a white inscription with black outlines "C" the size of your fist and say "C" out loud.
When you learn how to put a chord, you'll be putting it down already quickly.

6. Use your right thumb to alternate strumming the strings and check that all strings of the chord sound. If any string does not sound, check that the chord is correct. If all the strings sound, leave your thumb on the neck and bend the other fingers about 80%.

7. Taking into account the basic position of the hand for the chord C, repeat all over again from **step 1**.

If a string is muffled when it should be, you're:
* *Pressed the string far behind the metal strip or on the strip itself.* **Place your finger just behind the metal fret strip or in the middle of the fret.**
* *Slightly pressed the string.* **Hold it harder.**
* *Hitting the string with the other finger.* **Check, are your fingers arc-shaped? If not, make them arc-shaped. If the string is still muted, place the finger that strikes the string higher if it strikes the lower string or lower if it strikes the upper string.**
* *Little extended his palm out from under the neck.* **Bring your palm further out from under the neck.**

Do this exercise more than 10 times in a row. Rest and move on to the next exercise!

2.3. Exercise 5

Placing an Am and C chord with transposition of the ring finger

The Am and C chord have only 1 note difference. See how similar the Am and C chords are to each other.

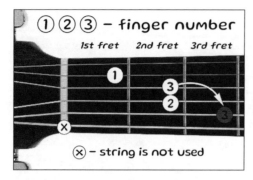

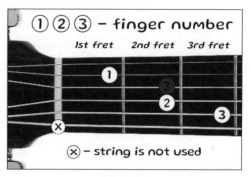

Transition from Am to C chord is made in 3 steps. **Step 2** and **step 3** are made at the moment of moving the finger to **step 1**.

1. When you have the chord Am set, lift your ring finger off the 3rd string and place the tip of your finger on the 5th string at the 3rd fret just behind the metal strip (or in the middle of the fret, if you don't have enough stretch). If the 4th string is muted, check to see if the pad of your ring finger is touching the 3rd string. If so, place your ring finger higher on the 5th string and move your palm further out from under the neck.

While you're repositioning your ring finger you need to:

2. Do everything that was described in "basic hand position for C chord" - **page 76**. I.e. by rotating the middle of the palm under the guitar neck and press the place where the thumb starts on the palm to the guitar neck to increase the amplitude of stretching the fingers for setting the C chord.

3. The middle finger, while keeping pressure on the string, slides from the middle of the fret to the right, closer to the metal strip of the 2nd fret.

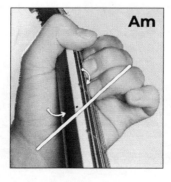

Am

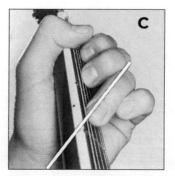

C

Important! You may find that you lack the stretch and fine motor skills to place your ring finger on the 3rd fret. This is normal, because small muscles need to be developed with practice! In this case, you can help your right hand to place the fingers of your left hand.

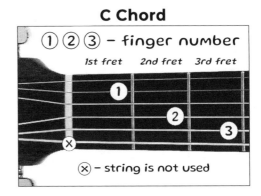

1. Perform the chord placement of Am.
2. Alternate strumming the strings with your right hand to check that all strings are sounding (if necessary, correct the fingers of your left hand to make the chord sound).
3. Raise your ring finger and start moving it to the 3rd fret of the 5th string behind the metal fret strip, at the same time with a rotating movement put the middle of your palm under the guitar neck, press the base of the thumb on the palm to the neck and move the middle finger on the 4th string from the middle of the 2nd fret to the right, closer to the metal fret strip.
4. Alternate strumming the strings with your right hand to check that all strings are sounding (if necessary, correct the fingers of your left hand to make the chord sound).
5. Play the Am chord again. To do this, lift your ring finger and move it to the 2nd fret of the 3rd string, while moving the base of your thumb away from the neck (as in the basic hand position for the Am pt X chord) and move your middle finger on the 4th string back to the middle of the 2nd fret.
6. Repeat from step 2.

The criterion for practicing the exercise a minimum of 50 times so that you can quickly transpose the chord.

2.3. Ex.5

🎓 **2.3. Exercise 6**

In this exercise we play in the first part all the same things we played in 2.3. exercise 3, and in the second part we add a C chord (you have already practiced transposing the ring finger from the Am chord to the C chord). Note that now the exercise consists of 4 circles.

The finger change is done in the same way as in 2.3. exercise 3 between 6 and 1 counts.

Exercise:

2.3. Ex.6

	Am	Asus 2	Am	C
1st string				
2nd string	1	0	1	1
3rd string	2 2	2 2	2 2	0 0
4th string	2 2	2 2	2 2	2 2
5th string	0	0	0	3
6th string				

Play fingerpicking on these chords.

If a string is muffled when it should be, you're:
- *Pressed the string far behind the metal strip or on the strip itself.* **Place your finger just behind the metal fret strip or in the middle of the fret.**
- *Slightly pressed the string.* **Hold it harder.**
- *Hitting the string with the other finger.* **Check, are your fingers arc-shaped? If not, make them arc-shaped. If the string is still muted, place the finger that strikes the string higher if it strikes the lower string or lower if it strikes the upper string.**
- *Little extended his palm out from under the neck.* **Bring your palm further out from under the neck.**

When you play this exercise for a total of 1.5 hours of pure playing, you will have mastered the transitions between chords and fingerpicking technique quite well.
The criterion for moving on is that you feel comfortable playing this exercise and you play it rhythmically, i.e. you pluck the strings at approximately the same interval of time.

P.S. When you are resting after playing any fingerpicking, practice setting other chords in **2.3. exercises 7 - 25.**

2.3.H

Why you should play 2.3. exercises 7 - 25 and when to proceed to chapter "2.4. Chords classification on the guitar"

Exercises **2.3. exercises 7 - 25** are necessary for you to memorize your finger placement and to quickly and easily place and rearrange your fingers in basic chords. In the future, you will be able to play almost any song on these chords, so it is very important to practice these exercises. Also, the songs at the end of this book will use all the chords that are practiced in these exercises, so if you skip the exercises, you will spend a very long time playing the songs, 1 minute, 2 minutes, rearranging them. Making transitions between chords 20,30, 40 seconds or more. I.e. it will be not playing songs, but picking the guitar. So all these exercises should be practiced so that you can play songs easily and with pleasure.

To master the material in chapter "**2.4 Classification of Chords on the Guitar**," you need to have at least some initial experience with the chords practiced in exercises 5-25. To get primary experience you need to play at least 20 times each exercise.
Also, all further materials of the book will be based on these same chords.

Practice all the chords from these exercises every day for at least 2 weeks.
The principle of the exercises will be the same.

In one series of exercises, you'll need to:
* Place the chord
* Check that the strings involved in the chord are sounding
* Remove your fingers from the strings
* Play the same chord or another chord with your fingers at the same time.

In another series of exercises, you'll need to:
* Place the chord
* Check that the strings involved in the chord are sounding
* Immediately play the next chord.

2.3. Exercise 7

Placing an Am + C chord with finger lifts from all strings

1. Play the basic hand position for the Am chord (**page 68**).
2. In your imagination, visualize bending each finger to the place where it should be on the string in an Am chord (as in "finger placement for Am chords" steps 1, 2, 3 - **page 68**).
3. In your imagination, visualize that you have already placed your fingers on the strings and strum the Am chord, and visualize above your fingers a white lettering with black outlines "Am" the size of your fist.
4. In reality, move the fingers of your left hand slowly and simultaneously and clamp the strings of the Am chord. Again over your fingers visualize the inscription "Am" and say "**Am**" out loud.
5. Check that all the strings sound (if necessary, correct your fingers so that all the strings of the chord sound).
6. Except for your thumb, spread the fingers of your left hand about 80% apart
7. Play the basic hand position for a C chord (**page 76**).
8. In your imagination, visualize bending each finger to where it should be on the string in a C chord (as in "finger placement for a C chord" steps 1, 2, 3 - **page 77**).
9. In your imagination, visualize how you have already placed your fingers on the strings and strum the C chord, and visualize above your fingers a white lettering with black outlines "C" the size of your fist.
10. In reality, slowly and simultaneously move the fingers of your left hand and clamp the strings of the chord C. Again over your fingers imagine the inscription "C" and say "C" out loud.
11. Check that all the strings sound (if necessary, correct your fingers so that all the strings of the chord sound).
12. Except for your thumb, spread the fingers of your left hand about 80%.
13. Repeat everything from **step 1**.

P.S. I give exercises on full chord placement specifically so that in the future when playing you can place chords very quickly and easily! Believe me, when you practice all this you will play very cool!
   Do this exercise 10 times in a row and you can move on to the next one.
   Practice this exercise at least a total of 50 times (not necessarily in 1 time, it can be several days).

2.3. Ex.7

2.3. Exercise 8

Placing a G Chord

The G chord has a similar shape to the C chord. Look at the left-hand drawing of the C chord shape. In the C chord, the index finger is on the next fret to the left of the middle finger and it is below the middle finger. In a G chord, the index finger is on the next fret to the left and is below the middle finger. In the G chord, the ring finger just shifts to the lower string. In the G chord, all 6 strings are used.

C Chord

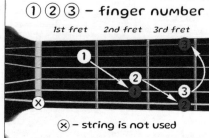

G Chord

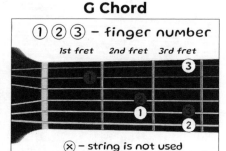

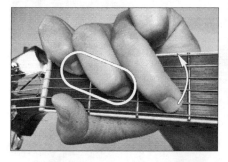

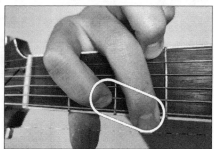

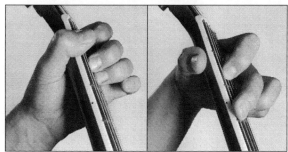

See what the bend in the hand joint looks like on the Am chord (left) and the G chord (right). You can see how in the G chord the hand is bent and the arm is extended slightly forward at the bend in the hand. This is to make it comfortable to place your fingers in the G chord.

Basic hand position for a G chord

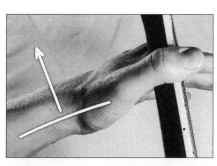

1. Place the pad of your left thumb on the neck above the metal metal fret strip of the 1st fret below the 6th string.

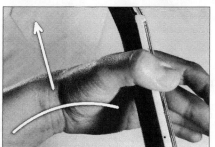

2. Bend the hand and bring the bend toward the neck head.

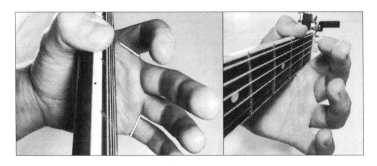

3. Move the palm of your hand forward from under the neck (as in "General Principles of chord placement with the left hand," - **page 66**).

Finger placement in a G chord:

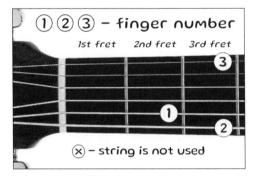

① ② ③ – finger number

1st fret   2nd fret   3rd fret

ⓧ – string is not used

1. Look at the 6th string just behind the metal strip on the 3rd fret. Imagine bending your middle finger and placing the bottom of your fingertip on the 6th string just behind the metal fret strip on the 3rd fret.

2. Look at the 5th string just behind the metal strip of the 2nd fret. Imagine bending your index finger and placing the bottom of your fingertip on the 5th string just behind the 2nd fret metal strip.

3. Look at the 1st string just behind the metal strip of the 3rd fret. Imagine bending your ring finger and placing your fingertip on the 1st string just behind the metal strip on the 3rd fret.

4. Imagine in your mind how you have already placed the entire G chord. The lower part of your middle finger tip is on the 6th string just behind the metal strip on the 3rd fret. The tip of your index finger is on the 5th string just behind the metal fret of the 2nd fret. The tip of the ring finger is on the 1st string just behind the metal strip of the 3rd fret. Above your fingers, visualize a white lettering with black outlines "G" the size of your fist.

5. In reality, begin to slowly* and simultaneously bend your middle, index, and ring fingers, moving them to the places on the strings where you have already clamped them in your imagination for the G chord. When you have clamped the strings again, visualize a white lettering with black outlines of "G" the size of your fist and say "**G**" out loud.

* When you learn a chord, you'll learn it fast. Slow is just for learning.

6. Use your right hand to alternate strum the strings and check that all the strings of the chord sound. If any string does not sound, check that the chord is correctly placed. If all the strings sound, leave your thumb on the neck and bend the other fingers about 80%.

7. Do it all over again from **step 1**.

If a string is muffled when it should be, you're:

- *Pressed the string far behind the metal strip or on the strip itself.* **Place your finger just behind the metal fret strip or in the middle of the fret.**
- *Slightly pressed the string.* **Hold it harder.**
- *Hitting the string with the other finger.* **Check, are your fingers arc-shaped? If not, make them arc-shaped. If the string is still muted, place the finger that strikes the string higher if it strikes the lower string or lower if it strikes the upper string.**
- *Little extended his palm out from under the neck.* **Bring your palm further out from under the neck.**

2.3. Exercise 9

Placing a C to G Chord

1. Play the basic hand position for the C chord (**page 76**).
2. In your imagination, visualize bending each finger to the place where it should be on the string in a C chord (as in "finger placement for a C chord" steps 1,2,3 - **page 77**).
3. In your imagination, visualize that you have already put your fingers on the strings and strum the C chord, and visualize above your fingers a white lettering with black outlines "C" the size of your fist.
4. In reality, slowly and simultaneously move the fingers of your left hand and clamp the strings of the chord C. So above your fingers imagine the inscription "C" and say aloud "C".
5. Check that all the strings sound (if necessary, correct your fingers so that all the strings of the chord sound).
6. Except for your thumb, spread the fingers of your left hand about 80% apart.
7. Play the basic hand position for the G chord (**page 82**).
8. In your imagination, visualize bending each finger to the place where it should be on the string in the G chord (as in "finger placement for the G chord" steps 1, 2, 3 - **page 83**).
9. In your imagination, visualize that you have already put your fingers on the strings and strum the G chord and imagine a white lettering with black outlines of "G" above your fingers the size of your fist.
10. In reality, move the fingers of your left hand slowly and simultaneously and clamp the strings of the G chord. Again over your fingers visualize the inscription "G" and say "G" out loud.
11. Check that all the strings sound (if necessary, correct your fingers so that all the strings of the chord sound).
12. Except for your thumb, spread the fingers of your left hand about 80%.
13. Repeat everything from **step 1**.

2.3. Exercise 10

Placing a D chord

I hope you've memorized the basic rules of chord placement by now:
- Clamp the strings 2-3 mm away from the metal fret strip (sometimes in the middle of the fret if your fingers are in the way).
- Move your palm out from under the neck so that there is more distance between your fingers and the neck.
- If something doesn't sound, it means that you are either holding the string loosely or muting it with a neighboring finger.

Basic hand position for a D chord:

The same as in the Am chord, except that the thumb is placed over the metal metal strip of the second fret (i.e., the whole position of the hand relative to Am chord is shifted to the right by 1 fret).

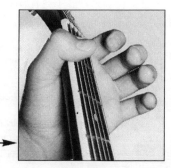

In Am it was like this ——————➤

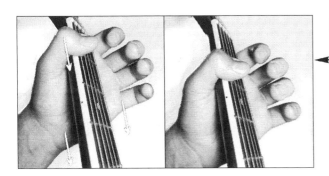

In D shifted the entire hand by 1 fret

D Chord

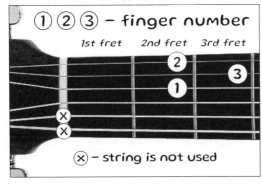

① ② ③ – finger number

1st fret   2nd fret   3rd fret

ⓧ – string is not used

Finger placement in a D chord:

1. Look at the 3rd string in the middle of the 2nd fret. Imagine bending your index finger and placing your fingertip on the 3rd string in the middle of the 2nd fret.
2. Look at the 2nd string just behind the metal strip on the 3rd fret. Imagine bending your ring finger and placing your fingertip on the 3rd string just behind the metal strip on the 3rd fret.
3. Look at the 1st string just behind the metal strip of the 2nd fret. Imagine bending your middle finger and placing your fingertip on the 1st string just behind the metal strip of the 2nd fret.
4. Imagine in your mind how you have already placed the entire D chord. The tip of your index finger is on the 3rd string in the middle of the 2nd fret. The tip of your ring finger is on the 2nd string just behind the metal strip on the 3rd fret. The tip of the middle finger is on the 1st string just behind the metal strip of the 2nd fret. Above your fingers, visualize a white lettering with black outlines "D" the size of your fist.
5. In reality, begin to slowly and simultaneously bend your middle, index, and ring fingers, moving them to the places on the strings where you have already clamped them in your imagination for the D chord. When you have clamped the strings again, visualize a white lettering with black outlines "D" the size of your fist and say "**D**" out loud.
6. Use your right thumb to alternate strumming the strings and check that all the strings of the chord sound. If any string does not sound, check that the chord is correct. If all the strings sound, leave your thumb on the neck and bend the other fingers about 80%.
7. Do it all over again from **step 1**.

Practice this exercise a total of at least 50 times.

🎓 2.3. Exercise 11

Placing a D - C Chord

1. Play the basic hand position for the D chord (**page 84**).
2. In your imagination, visualize bending each finger to the place where it should be on the string for a D chord (as in "finger placement for a D chord" steps 1, 2, 3 - **page 85**).
3. In your imagination, visualize that you have already placed your fingers on the strings and strum the D chord, and visualize above your fingers a white lettering with black outlines "D" the size of your fist.
4. In reality, move the fingers of your left hand slowly and simultaneously and clamp the strings of the D chord. Again over your fingers visualize the inscription "D" and say "**D**" out loud.
5. Check that all the strings sound (if necessary, correct your fingers so that all the strings of the chord sound).
6. In addition to your thumb, spread the fingers of your left hand about 80% apart
7. Play the basic hand position for a C chord (**page 76**).
8. In your imagination, visualize bending each finger to where it should be on the string in a C chord (as in "finger placement for a C chord" steps 1, 2, 3 - **page 77**).
9. In your imagination, visualize that you have already placed your fingers on the strings and strum the C chord and imagine a white lettering with black outlines of "C" above your fingers the size of your fist.
10. In reality, slowly and simultaneously move the fingers of your left hand and clamp the strings of the chord C. Again above your fingers imagine the inscription "C" and say "**C**" out loud.
11. Check that all the strings sound (if necessary, correct your fingers so that all the strings of the chord sound).
12. Except for your thumb, spread the fingers of your left hand about 80% apart.
13. Repeat everything from **step 1**.

Practice this exercise a total of at least 50 times.

2.3. Ex.11

🎓 2.3. Exercise 12

Placing a D - G Chord

1. Play the basic hand position for the D chord (**page 84**).
2. In your imagination, visualize bending each finger to the place where it should be on the string for a D chord (as in "finger placement for a D chord" steps 1, 2, 3 - **page 85**).
3. In your imagination, visualize that you have already placed your fingers on the strings and strum the D chord, and visualize above your fingers a white lettering with black outlines "D" the size of your fist.
4. In reality, move the fingers of your left hand slowly and simultaneously and clamp the strings of the D chord. Again over your fingers visualize the inscription "D" and say "**D**" out loud.
5. Check that all the strings sound (if necessary, correct your fingers so that all the strings of the chord sound).

6. In addition to your thumb, spread the fingers of your left hand about 80% apart
7. Play the basic hand position for the G chord (**page 82**).
8. In your imagination, visualize bending each finger to the place where it should be on the string in the G chord (as in "finger placement for the G chord" steps 1, 2, 3 - **page 83**).
9. In your imagination, visualize that you have already put your fingers on the strings and strum the G chord and imagine a white lettering with black outlines of "G" above your fingers the size of your fist.
10. In reality, move the fingers of your left hand slowly and simultaneously and clamp the strings of the G chord. Again over your fingers visualize the inscription "G" and say "**G**" out loud.
11. Check that all the strings sound (if necessary, correct your fingers so that all the strings of the chord sound).
12. Except for your thumb, spread the fingers of your left hand about 80%.
13. Repeat everything from **step 1**.

Practice this exercise a total of at least 50 times.

2.3. Ex.12

🎓 **2.3. Exercise 13**

Placing a D - C - D - G Chord

Only go to this exercise when you have already practiced the previous exercises in chapter 2.3.

This exercise combines 3 chords that you have already mastered. In fact, you can play a full song on them later!

1. Given a basic hand position, place a D chord
2. Check the sound of the chord
3. Flex the fingers of your left hand except for the thumb
4. Given the basic hand position, play a C chord
5. Check the sound of the chord
6. Flex the fingers of your left hand except for the thumb
7. Given the basic hand position, play a D chord
8. Check the sound of the chord
9. Flex the fingers of your left hand except for the thumb
10. Given the basic hand position, play a G chord
11. Check the sound of the chord
12. Flex the fingers of your left hand except for the thumb
13. Repeat **step 1**.

2.3. Ex.13

Continuing to learn chords, there are 4 more chords left to learn and your arsenal of chords will cover almost all songs! Master their placement and we'll move on to fingerpicking on these chords.

2.3.1

How to quickly learn chord placement and how to practice exercises 14-25

Let's highlight the basic chord memorization scheme. You've probably already figured it out, but I want to separate it out and make it universal. When you learn new chords, for example, in the second book of my series of guitar teaching books or anywhere else, I recommend that you use this method to quickly memorize a chord:

1. You look at the chord diagram to see where which finger should stand.
2. You put your left hand on the guitar neck in the basic position.
3. Look at the string and fret where your finger should stand.
4. Imagine bending your finger and placing it on that string on that fret.
5. Repeat step 3 with the rest of the strings and fingers.
6. Imagine putting all your fingers in the right places and visualize the name of the chord above the hand.
7. In reality, slowly* and simultaneously move all fingers to the strings and press them down. (*slowly only while learning).
8. Again visualize the chord name over the hand and say the chord name out loud.

2.3. Exercise 14

Placing a Dm Chord

Dm Chord

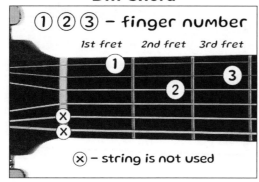

The basic hand position for the Dm chord is the same as for the C chord (page 76).

Finger placement in a Dm chord:

1. Look at the 3rd string just behind the metal strip on the 2nd fret. Imagine bending your middle finger and placing your fingertip on the 3rd string just behind the metal strip on the 2nd fret.
2. Look at the 2nd string just behind the metal strip of the 3rd fret. Imagine bending your ring finger and placing your fingertip on the 3rd string just behind the metal strip of the 3rd fret.
3. Look at the 1st string just behind the metal strip of the 1st fret. Imagine bending your index finger and placing your fingertip on the 1st string just behind the metal strip on the 1st fret.

4. Imagine in your mind how you have already placed the entire Dm chord. The tip of your middle finger is on the 3rd string just behind the metal fret of the 2nd fret. The tip of your ring finger is on the 2nd string just behind the metal strip on the 3rd fret. The tip of the index finger is on the 1st string just behind the metal strip of the 1st fret. Above your fingers, imagine a white lettering with black outlines "Dm" the size of your fist.

5. In reality, begin to slowly and simultaneously bend your middle, index, and ring fingers, moving them to the places on the strings where you have already clamped them in your imagination for the Dm chord. When you've clamped the strings again, visualize a white lettering with black outlines "Dm" the size of your fist and say "**Dm**" out loud.

6. Use your right thumb to alternate strumming the strings and check that all the strings of the chord are sounding. If any string does not sound, check that the chord is correct. If all the strings sound, leave your thumb on the neck and bend the other fingers about 80%.

7. Do it all over again from **step 1**.

The criterion for good practice is to have performed the Dm chord placement more than 50 times.

2.3. Exercise 15

Placing a Dm - Am Chord

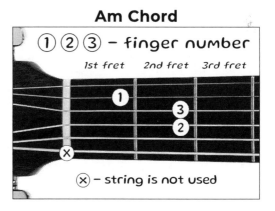

1. Given a basic hand position, place the chord Dm
2. Check the sound of the chord
3. Flex the fingers of your left hand except for the thumb
4. Given the basic hand position, play an Am chord
5. Check the sound of the chord
6. Flex the fingers of your left hand except for the thumb
7. Repeat everything from **step 1**.

2.3. Ex.15

2.3. Exercise 16

Placing an Em chord

Em Chord

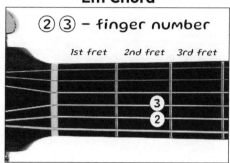

The basic hand position for an Em chord is the same as for an Am chord except that the thumb is lower behind the neck to allow the 6th string to vibrate (**page 68**).

Finger placement in the Em chord:
1. Look at the 5th string in the middle of the 2nd fret. Imagine bending your middle finger and placing your fingertip on the 5th string in the middle of the 2nd fret.
2. Look at the 4th string just behind the metal strip on the 2nd fret. Imagine bending your ring finger and placing your fingertip on the 4th string just behind the metal strip on the 2nd fret.
3. Imagine in your mind how you have already placed the entire Em chord. The tip of your middle finger is on the 5th string in the middle of the 2nd fret. The tip of your ring finger is on the 4th string just behind the metal strip on the 2nd fret. Above your fingers, visualize a white lettering with black outlines "Em" the size of your fist.
4. In reality, begin to bend your middle and ring fingers slowly and simultaneously, moving them to the places on the strings where you have already clamped them in your imagination for the Em chord. When you have clamped the strings again, imagine a white lettering with black outlines "Em" the size of your fist and say "**Em**" out loud.
5. With your right thumb, swipe the strings alternately and check that all the strings of the chord are sounding. If any string does not sound, check that the chord is correct. If all the strings sound, leave your thumb on the neck and bend the other fingers about 80%.
6. Do it all over again from **step 1**.

2.3. Exercise 17

Placing an Am - Em Chord

Am Chord

Em Chord

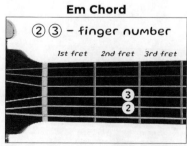

1. Put an Am chord in the chord
2. Check the sound of the chord
3. Flex the fingers of your left hand except for the thumb
4. Play the Em chord
5. Check the sound of the chord
6. Flex the fingers of your left hand except the thumb and repeat from **step 1**.

Placing an E chord

E Chord

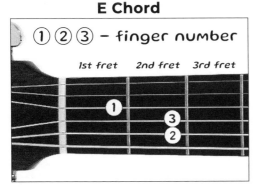

① ② ③ – finger number

1st fret   2nd fret   3rd fret

The basic hand position for an E chord is the same as for an Am chord except that the thumb is lower behind the neck to allow the 6th string to vibrate (**page 68**).

Finger placement in the E chord:

1. Finger placement in the E chord.
2. Look at the 5th string in the middle of the 2nd fret. Imagine bending your middle finger and placing your fingertip on the 5th string in the middle of the 2nd fret.
3. Look at the 4th string just behind the metal strip on the 2nd fret. Imagine bending your ring finger and placing your fingertip on the 4th string just behind the metal strip on the 2nd fret.
4. Look at the 3rd string just behind the metal strip of the 1st fret. Imagine bending your index finger and placing your fingertip on the 3rd string just behind the metal strip on the 1st fret.
5. Imagine in your mind how you have already placed the entire Em chord. The tip of your middle finger is on the 5th string in the middle of the 2nd fret. The tip of your ring finger is on the 4th string just behind the metal strip on the 2nd fret. The tip of the index finger is on the 3rd string just behind the metal strip on the 1st fret. Above your fingers, visualize a white lettering with black outlines "E" the size of your fist.
6. In reality, begin to slowly and simultaneously bend your middle, ring and index fingers, moving them to the places on the strings where you have already clamped them in your imagination for the E chord. When you have clamped the strings again, visualize a white lettering with black outlines "E" the size of your fist and say "**E**" out loud.
7. Use your right thumb to stroke the strings alternately and check that all the strings of the chord are sounding. If any string does not sound, check that the chord is correct. If all the strings sound, leave your thumb on the neck and bend the other fingers about 80%.
8. Do it all over again from **step 1**.

2.3. Exercise 19

Placing an Am - E Chord

1. Put an Am chord in the chord
2. Check the sound of the chord
3. Flex the fingers of your left hand except for the thumb
4. Play the E chord
5. Check the sound of the chord
6. Flex the fingers of your left hand except for the thumb
7. Repeat everything from **step 1**.

2.3. Ex.19

2.3. Exercise 20

In this chord, it is physically impossible to put each finger immediately behind the metal strip, so the fingers are placed diagonally.

A Chord

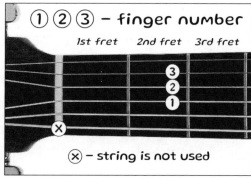

The basic hand position for chord A is the same as for chord G (**page 82**).

Finger placement in the A chord:
1. Look at the 4th string at the end of the 2nd fret (at the fret strip of the 1st fret). Imagine bending your index finger and placing your fingertip on the 4th string at the end of the 2nd fret.
2. Look at the 3rd string right in the middle of the 2nd fret. Imagine bending your middle finger and placing your fingertip on the 3rd string in the middle of the 2nd fret.
3. Look at the 2nd string just behind the metal strip of the 2nd fret. Imagine bending your ring finger and placing your fingertip on the 2nd string just behind the metal strip on the 2nd fret.
4. Imagine in your mind how you have already placed the entire chord A. The tip of your index finger is on the 4th string at the end of the 2nd fret. The tip of your middle finger is on the 3rd string in the middle of the 2nd fret. The tip of the ring finger is on the 2nd string just behind the metal strip on the 2nd fret. Above your fingers, visualize a white lettering with black outlines "A" the size of your fist.
5. In reality, start bending your middle and ring fingers slowly and simultaneously, moving them to the places on the strings where you have already clamped them in your imagination to set the chord A. When you have clamped the strings again, imagine a white inscription with black outlines "A" the size of your fist and say "**A**" out loud.

6. Use your right thumb to stroke the strings alternately and check that all the strings of the chord are sounding. If any string does not sound, check that the chord is correct. If all the strings sound, leave your thumb on the neck and bend the other fingers about 80%.
7. Do it all over again from **step 1**.

You can stop visualizing the chord name and pronouncing the chord name when you immediately remember how to place the chord. This will happen after about 15-50 times of playing each chord.

2.3. Exercise 21

Placing an A - E Chord

1. Place the A chord
2. Check the sound of the chord
3. Flex the fingers of your left hand except for the thumb
4. Place the E chord
5. Check the sound of the chord
6. Flex the fingers of your left hand except for the thumb
7. Repeat everything from **step 1**.

2.3. Ex.21

2.3. Exercise 22

Placing an A - D Chord

1. Place the A chord
2. Check the sound of the chord
3. Flex the fingers of your left hand except for the thumb
4. Place the D chord
5. Check the sound of the chord
6. Flex the fingers of your left hand except for the thumb
7. Repeat everything from **step 1**.

2.3. Ex.22

2.3. Exercise 23

Placing an A - G Chord

1. Place the A chord
2. Check the sound of the chord
3. Flex the fingers of your left hand except for the thumb
4. Place the G chord
5. Check the sound of the chord
6. Flex the fingers of your left hand except for the thumb
7. Repeat everything from **step 1**.

2.3. Ex.23

2.3. Exercise 24

Placing an Em - C Chord

2.3. Ex.24

1. Place the Em chord
2. Check the sound of the chord
3. Flex the fingers of your left hand except for the thumb
4. Place the C chord
5. Check the sound of the chord
6. Flex the fingers of your left hand except for the thumb
7. Repeat everything from **step 1**.

 2.3. Exercise 25

Placing an Em - G Chord

2.3. Ex.25

1. Place the Em chord
2. Check the sound of the chord
3. Flex the fingers of your left hand except for the thumb
4. Place the G chord
5. Check the sound of the chord
6. Flex the fingers of your left hand except for the thumb
7. Repeat everything from **step 1**.

2.4. GUITAR CHORD CLASSIFICATION

We've learned the basic chords that almost every song in the world is based on! Now let's learn how to navigate these chords on the guitar and how to play them.

There are chords that start on the 4,5 and 6 strings. Why they are from 4,5 and 6 strings we will study in the next book, in which we will study with you how chords are built, how to move chords from one position to another, how to play the same chord in different places of the guitar neck and many other interesting topics and exercises.

We've been learning the chords:
* from the 4th string - **Dm, D**
* from the 5th string - **Am, A, C**
* from the 6th string - **E, Em, G, F**.

Now to easily play fingerpicking on these chords, we need to memorize a very simple basic fingerpicking pattern.

BASIC PATTERNS OF FINGERPICKING STRINGS

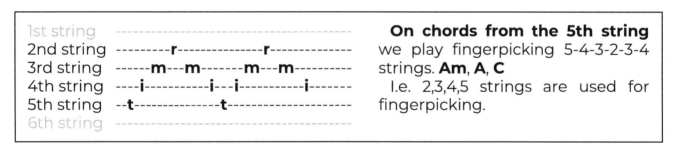

```
1st string  ----------r--------------r------------
2nd string  ------m---m-------m---m----------
3rd string  ----i----------i---i----------i-------
4th string  --t-------------t-------------------
4th string  ...................................
6th string  ...................................
```

On chords from the 4th string we play fingerpicking 4-3-2-1-2-3 strings. **Dm, D**
I.e. 1,2,3,4 strings are used for fingerpicking.

```
1st string  ...................................
2nd string  ----------r--------------r-------------
3rd string  ------m---m-------m---m----------
4th string  ----i----------i---i----------i-------
5th string  --t-------------t-------------------
6th string  ...................................
```

On chords from the 5th string we play fingerpicking 5-4-3-2-3-4 strings. **Am, A, C**
I.e. 2,3,4,5 strings are used for fingerpicking.

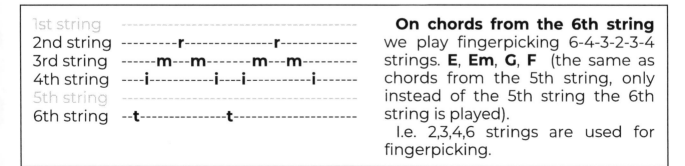

```
1st string  ...................................
2nd string  ----------r--------------r-------------
3rd string  ------m---m-------m---m----------
4th string  ----i----------i---i----------i-------
5th string  ...................................
6th string  --t-------------t-------------------
```

On chords from the 6th string we play fingerpicking 6-4-3-2-3-4 strings. **E, Em, G, F** (the same as chords from the 5th string, only instead of the 5th string the 6th string is played).
I.e. 2,3,4,6 strings are used for fingerpicking.

All of these chord sequences are used in so many songs, so by practicing them, you are actually playing the song. You just need to add vocals and the song is ready.

Before proceeding to the next exercises, please reread the description and do the following exercises again to remember fingerpicking and chord changes.
- 2.3. Exercise 2 (**page 72**) - play for 2 minutes
- 2.3. Exercise 3 (**page 74**) - play for 2 minutes
- 2.3. Exercise 6 (**page 79**) - play for 2 minutes

2.4. Exercise 1

Play a basic pattern of fingerpicking strings on the G chord for 3 minutes to prepare for the following exercises.

```
1st string  --------------------------------------
2nd string  -------0----------0------
3rd string  -----0--0------0--0----
4th string  ---0------0--0------0--
4th string  --------------------------------------
6th string  -3----------3------------
```

2.4. Exercise 2

Fingerpicking on chords G - C - D - G

This exercise is the same as the ones I asked you to repeat (2.3 Exercises 2,3,6), only in fingerpicking you will play other strings, according to pattern I described earlier - **BASIC PATTERNS OF FINGERPICKING STRINGS**.

Pay attention to your right hand. When you change the fingerpicking position from 4-3-2-1 strings to 6-4-3-2 strings, your right hand just shifts vertically, i.e. you just shift the position of the lower bone of your palm. I mentioned this in 2.2. Exercise 2 (**page 54**).

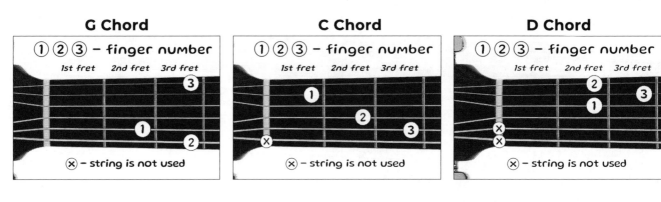

```
                G                    C                    D                    G
1st string  -------------------------------------------0---------0------------------------
2nd string  -------0----------0---------1----------1--------3--3-----3--3--------0----------0-----
3rd string  -----0--0------0--0------0--0------0--0----2------2--2-----2---0--0------0--0---
4th string  ---0------0--0------0--2------2--2------2-0------0---------0------0--0------0-
5th string  -----------------------3----------3------------------------------------------
6th string  -3----------3------------------------------------3----------3-----------
```

2.4. Ex.2

Loop this exercise by playing it in a circle G, C, D, G - G, C, D, G - G, C, D, G …
The criterion for good practice of 2.4. Exercises 2-5 - you play fingerpicking and chord changes without jerking, the sound is even and rhythmic (no stops).

2.4. Exercise 3

Fingerpicking on chords Em - C - G - D

Em Chord

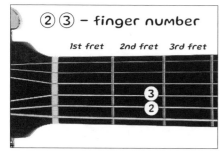

② ③ – finger number

1st fret 2nd fret 3rd fret

③
②

String fingerpicking using a pattern (basic patterns of fingerpicking strings).

2.4. Ex.3

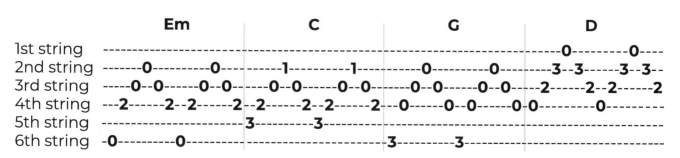

```
             Em              C               G               D
1st string  ----------------------------------------------------------0--------0----
2nd string  ------0----------0----1----------1----0----------0----3--3----3--3--
3rd string  ----0--0------0--0--0--0------0--0--0--0------0--0--2------2--2------2
4th string  ---2------2--2------2--2------2--2------2--0------0--0------0--0--------0----
5th string  ----------------------3----------3----------------------------------
6th string  -0----------0--------------------------3----------3----------------------
```

Loop this exercise by playing it again and again.

2.4. Exercise 4

Fingerpicking on chords Am - C - Dm - G

String fingerpicking using a pattern (basic patterns of fingerpicking strings).

Am Chord

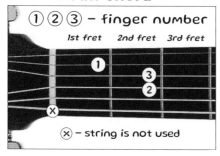

① ② ③ – finger number

1st fret 2nd fret 3rd fret

①
③
②
⊗

⊗ – string is not used

Dm Chord

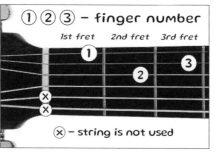

① ② ③ – finger number

1st fret 2nd fret 3rd fret

①
③
②
⊗
⊗

⊗ – string is not used

2.4. Ex.4

```
             Am              C               Dm              G
1st string  --------------------------------------------1----------1--------------------
2nd string  ------1----------1----1----------1----3--3----3--3----0----------0-----
3rd string  ----2--2------2--2--0--0------0--0--2------2--2------2--0--0------0--0---
4th string  ---2------2--2------2--2------2--2------2-0----------0----------0--0--------0-
5th string  -0----------0----3----------3----------------------------------
6th string  ------------------------------------------------------3----------3----------
```

Loop this exercise by playing it again and again.

2.4. Exercise 5

Fingerpicking on chords Am - Dm - E - Am

String fingerpicking using a pattern (basic patterns of fingerpicking strings).

Am Chord
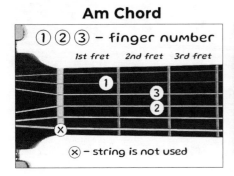

Dm Chord
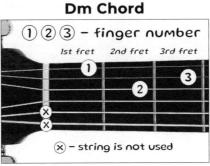

E Chord
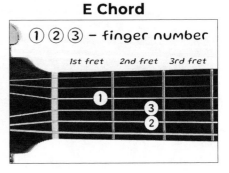

	Am	Dm	E	Am
1st string	-----------------------------	---1---------1---	-----------------------	------------------
2nd string	-------1----------1--------	--3--3-----3--3-------	---0---------0----	-------1---------1----
3rd string	----2--2------2--2---	-2------2--2------2-----	1--1-----1--1---	--2--2------2--2--
4th string	---2------2--2-----2-0-------	---0------------------	--2----2--2----2--	--2--2------2--2------2
5th string	-0---------0-----------	-------------------------	-------------------0---------0---------
6th string	-----------------------------	-------------0---------0---------	---------------------

Loop this exercise by playing it again and again.

2.4. Ex.5

CHAPTER 3
STRUMMING

3.1

Right hand strumming on the guitar

This is a playing technique that supplements guitar playing with a percussion component. A huge number of songs in different styles are based on this playing technique. Almost all guitar playing consists of either fingerpicking and its variations or strumming and variations of strumming, so you should study strumming. It is a very interesting and beautiful guitar playing technique.

An important rule of strumming!
When striking the strings, strike only 2 or 3 strings. This allows you to make rhythmic accents and such a sound will be well intelligible. If you strumming on all 6 strings, you will have a mess of sounds that will sound disgusting.

You can safely hit different numbers of strings when playing strumming down and up. Playing down sometimes you can hit the 6th,5th,4th string and sometimes you can hit the 6th,5th. Playing upwards sometimes you can hit the 1st,2nd,3rd strings and sometimes the 1st,2nd strings. This unevenness creates a dynamic colouring of playing, a pleasant sound and accents in the rhythm. All this gives a nice variety in the performance!

Strumming is divided into 3 movements:
1. Downstroke (from thick strings to thin strings)
2. Upward strike (from thin strings to thick strings)
3. Dead note.

All these parts must first be worked out separately and then combined into one movement.

Right hand placement for strumming

If in fingerpicking the palm of the hand rests on the string holder, in strumming the hand is on the weight. The hand rests only with the forearm on the edge of the guitar body.

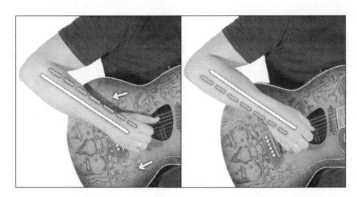

To put the right hand to play strumming you should put your hand in the same way as for fingerpicking, and then, lifting the right hand from the guitar with the left hand, move the guitar itself to the right about 2 inches. It's important to slide just the guitar, leaving the hand in place. If you leave the guitar in place and move your arm, you will change the angle in your shoulder and may get a slight tension in your shoulder muscles. That's why it's better to move the guitar.

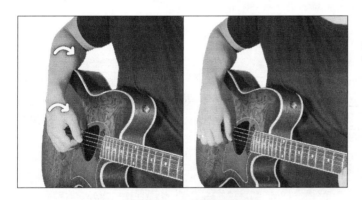

Next you need to rotate your forearm slightly anti-clockwise - to the left by about 15 degrees.

So your right hand should be over the area shown in the picture, this is the working area of strumming, this is the most comfortable place to play. If you play closer to the string holder, it will be hard to play because the strings are more tightly stretched and you need to apply more force. If you play closer to the neck, you can rub your fingers bloody, because your fingers will get caught (fall through) between the strings.

Therefore, you should play in the middle (+/- 2 inches) between the string holder and the beginning of the resonating hole.

3.2. STRUMMING. 1

Down kick

The downstroke is done with the right thumb. The point of contact between your thumb and the strings is about the same as when you pluck a string with your thumb when playing fingerpicking.

Striking the strings has 2 parts, which are done simultaneously:

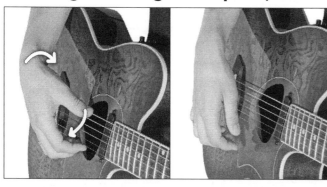

1. Bending the thumb towards the palm of the hand
2. Rotation of the hand anti-clockwise.

Bending the thumb plucks the strings, while counterclockwise rotation of the hand gives power to the thumb strike. In addition, both of these movements give an almost straight strike line perpendicular to the strings, which gives the most even sound.

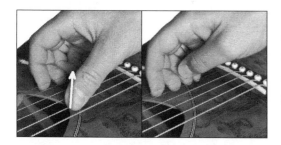

If you strike with the thumb only, the sound will be more muffled, because the thumb has rather little power compared to the forearm, and the line of movement of the thumb will be diagonal and the sound of the strings will be different.

Right now you can pluck, for example, the 4th string 1 inch from the bridge with your thumb. Then pluck the string where you normally pluck the string with your thumb when playing fingerpicking and pluck the string where the neck ends. And you'll hear that the sound is very different in its overtones.

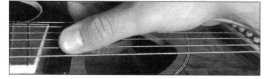

The bridge has a very ringing sound, over the neck it's very soft, and in the middle it's a medium sound.

The same goes for the upward punch with the index finger, which is combined with the rotation of the hand. It's like in boxing, where the real punch is not just with the arm, but starts with the leg, the momentum goes through the whole body and ends with the throwing out of the arm.

Let's move on to practising phase 1 of the movement.

The strumming is represented on the diagram by the up and down arrows. Remember that in the chord/tablature diagram, the 6th string is at the bottom and the 1st string is at the top?

Let's take the E chord as an example

E Chord

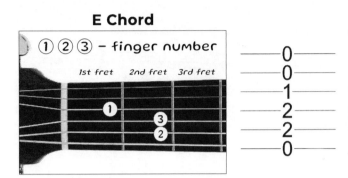

This is what an E chord looks like in tablature form. If you don't remember how the numbers appeared, read "2.3.J. How to Read Guitar Tablature" on **page 73**. Let me remind you. At the top of the tablature is the 1st string, which is thin. On the bottom of the tablature is the 6th string, which is thick. The number on the tablature means the number of the fret on which the string is clamped, where 0 is the open string.

Since in strumming, we only hit two or three strings when we strike, let's keep only the bottom of the E chord in the pattern.

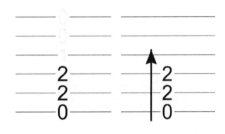

The up arrow on the diagram means that you should strike from the thick strings to the thin strings. I.e. with your right thumb you hit the **bass strings*** on the guitar from top to bottom, from the 6th to the 4th string.
   *Bass strings are 6,5 and 4 strings, they are wound with an additional ring braid and chords are built from them (from 4,5,6 strings).

Just in case, let me remind you that the up arrow on the tablature means the down beat on the guitar, because on the tablature the 6th string is at the bottom and the up arrow means the movement from the 6th to the 1st string. And in reality, the 6th string on the guitar is on top. The movement is the same, from the 6th to the 1st string, but it turns out that in reality on the guitar it is a downbeat.

Once again:
- Up arrow on tablature = downstroke on guitar (6 to 1 string)
- Down arrow on tablature = upstroke on guitar (1 to 6 strings).

3.2. Exercise 1

Strumming down ONLY with the thumb on the 6,5 and 4 strings

The purpose of this exercise is to get a feel for the movement of the thumb and how to strike the strings with it.

In this exercise you will practice strumming without rotating the hand, only by the movement of the thumb. All fingers of the right hand, except the thumb, relax and hold them over the strings.

- Place your right hand in the strumming position (right hand placement for strumming **page 100**)
- With your left hand, strum an E chord
1. Strike the 6th, 5th, and 4th strings with a quick sliding motion of your right thumb
2. Repeat **step 1** at regular intervals between beats.

Play the exercise for 1-3 minutes.

3.2. Ex.1

 3.2. Exercise 2

Everything is the same as the previous exercise, but now we add counterclockwise rotation of the hand.

At the same time, rotate the hand counterclockwise and bend the thumb while striking the 6th, 5th and 4th strings.

Mind you, you can hit two or three strings (6th, 5th or 6th, 5th, 4th strings).

Play this exercise until you feel that you can hit the strings easily with your thumb and hit the strings well without hitting the 4th or 3rd strings, but only the 6th,5th or 6th,5th and 4th strings. Make sure that the strings sound evenly, i.e. the 6th,5th and 4th strings sound about the same in volume.

3.2. Ex.2

3.2. STRUMMING. 2

Up kick

The upstroke is made with the index finger of the right hand. The point of contact between the index finger and the strings is about the same as where you pull the string with your index finger when playing fingerpicking strings.

VERY IMPORTANT - hitting the strings also consists of 2 components that are done simultaneously:

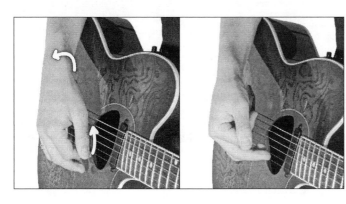

1. Bending the index finger toward the palm of the hand
2. Clockwise rotation of the hand.

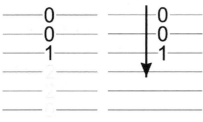

Let's continue on the same E chord.

Let's leave only the upper part of the chord E. The down arrow on the diagram means that you should strike from the thin strings to the thick strings, from the 1st string to the 3rd string. I.e. with the index finger of your right hand you hit the 1st, 2nd, 3rd strings from bottom to top.

 3.2. Exercise 3

Strumming upward ONLY with the index finger on the 1,2 and 3 strings

In this exercise we will practice strumming with movement, without rotation of the hand, using only the bending of the index finger. All fingers of the right hand, except the index finger, are relaxed and above strings.

- Place your right hand in the strumming position
- With your left hand, strum an E chord
1. Strike the 1st, 2nd, and 3rd strings with a quick sliding motion of the right index finger
2. Repeat **step 1** at regular intervals between beats.

Play the exercise for 1-3 minutes.

3.2. Ex.3

3.2. Exercise 4

It's the same as the previous exercise, but now we add clockwise rotation of the hand. Simultaneously rotate your hand clockwise and bend your index finger to strike the 1st, 2nd and 3rd strings.

Let me remind you that you don't have to try to hit all three strings (1st, 2nd, 3rd). You can hit two or three strings. 1st, 2nd or 1st, 2nd, 3rd strings.

Play this exercise until you feel that you can easily hit the 4th or 5th strings with your index finger along with the rotation of your hand. Also, make sure that when you strike the strings, the sound of the 1st, 2nd and 3rd strings is about the same volume. If one of the strings sounds louder than the others, it means that you are hitting that string harder and the others weaker, and you should hit the strings evenly.

3.2. Ex.4

3.2. Exercise 5

Combining downward and upward kick

* Place your right hand in the strumming position
* With your left hand, strum an E chord
1. Make a downstroke by rotating your hand counterclockwise and bending your thumb over the bass strings (6th, 5th, 4th or 6th, 5th-whatever works)
2. Strike upward by rotating the hand clockwise and bending the index finger over the thin strings (1st, 2nd, 3rd or 1st, 2nd-as you get it)
3. Repeat **step 1** at regular intervals between strokes.

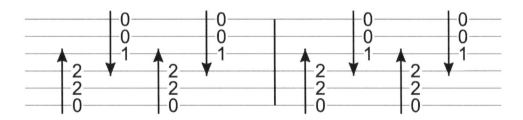

P.S. Note that it should not be that the downstroke is very loud and the upstroke is quiet or vice versa. The sound should be approximately equal in volume when hitting down and when hitting up.

Play this exercise until you feel that you are able to play without sudden jerks, i.e. rhythmically even, the sound volume is approximately the same and in general you feel comfortable playing this exercise. You can also vary the volume level of your playing by making stronger beats or, on the contrary, weaker beats.

* Example of poor playing volume and rhythm
* Example of good volume and rhythm playing

3.2. Ex.5

3.2. STRUMMING. 3

Dead note

It is this element in strumming that gives the feeling of playing percussion and emphasizes the rhythmic pattern! It also consists of two parts:
1. Striking the strings downward with your index finger (from the bass strings to the fine strings)
2. Dropping the bottom of the palm and the palm rib on the strings.

The dead note is simple enough to do. It's like flicking your index finger, as if you want to hit a breadcrumb on the table to make it fly away.

The index finger, stretched like a bowstring, strikes the strings. You should hit the 5th, 4th, 3rd, 2nd strings with your index finger. It may happen that you will hit other strings, but the main blow is in the area of the 5th, 4th, 3rd, 2nd strings. At the same time as the index finger strikes, the lower part of the palm of the hand falls on the strings to muffle them. It turns out that two sounds are put together. The palm of the hand strikes the strings and the index finger strikes the strings.

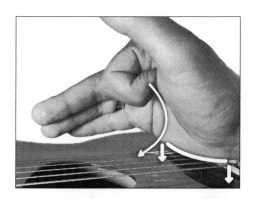  

3.2. Exercise 6

Dead note on the strings

- Place your right hand in the strumming position, and remove your left hand from the neck of the guitar so that the strings are open.

1. Make a dead note with your index finger downward, striking the 5th,4th,3rd,2nd strings with it and at the same time throw the bottom and rib of your palm against the strings.
2. Repeat step 1 at regular intervals between strokes.

If you hear the strings sounding at first and then they become muffled, it means that you are making the bottom of the palm and the palm rib drop after hitting the dead note. Your task is to simultaneously make a blow with your index finger and hit the strings with the bottom of the palm and the edge of the palm.

When you master this technique, move on to the next exercise, where we will combine all 3 elements of strumming.

In tablature, the dead note is labeled X (x - dead note / muted note).

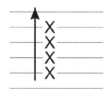

3.2. Ex.6

3.2. Exercise 7

Combining a downward, upward kick and a dead note

REMINDER!
Up arrow on tablature = downstroke on guitar (6th to 1st string)
Down arrow on tablature = upstroke on guitar (1st to 6th string)

The basic strumming pattern you are about to master consists of:
1. Thumb strike downward
2. Upward stroke with index finger
3. Dead note (muffled thumbs down punch)
4. Thump upward with index finger

To simplify:
1. down
2. up
3. dead note
4. up

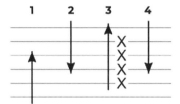

3.2. Ex.7

- Place your right hand in the strumming position
- With your left hand, strum an E chord
1. With your right thumb, strike down on the 6th, 5th, 4th strings.
2. With your index finger, strike upward on the 1st, 2nd, 3rd strings.
3. With your index finger, make a dead note on the 5th, 4th, 3rd, 2nd strings and at the same time strike the bottom and the edge of your palm on the strings.
4. Use your index finger to strike upward on the 1st, 2nd, 3rd strings.
5. Repeat **step 1** (loop the movement), keeping equal time intervals between blows.

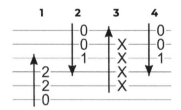

Congratulations, this is the basic rhythmic pattern of strumming! Now you need to practice this strumming on different chords and chord strings.

3.2. Exercise 8

Do the same as in the previous exercise (exercise 7), but on a **G** chord.

G Chord

① ② ③ – finger number

1st fret   2nd fret   3rd fret

③

①

②

ⓧ – string is not used

3.2. STRUMMING. 4

How to make chord changes when strumming

Very important!

When you change a chord, be sure to keep playing the strumming. You can't stop, even if you haven't gotten the chord right. It's the strumming that creates the rhythm, and if you stop, you'll get a break in the rhythm and it will sound terrible! The chord change is done on the last strike of the strings, when you play with your index finger up.

In this exercise, you will play 1 chord for 2 strumming circles.

1 round of strumming is: down, up, dead note, up.

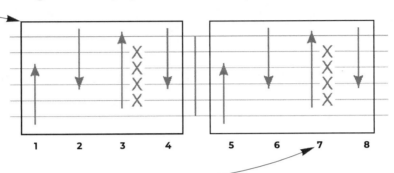

After the 7th kick (dead note):

1. You need to lift the fingers of your left hand off the strings.
2. Make the last (8th) strumming stroke with the right hand on the open strings.
3. Simultaneously with striking the strings with your right hand, start moving the fingers of your left hand to set a new chord, and by the time the first beat of the new strumming circle is struck, you should already have a new chord set.

3.2. Exercise 9

Playing Strumming on the Em - G Chord

Everything is the same as the previous two exercises (7 and 8), except now play strumming with a chord change. I remind you that 1 chord is played by 2 strumming circles (1 circle = down-up- dead note-up).

- Place the **Em** chord (carefully, not E, but specifically Em).
1. Start playing the strumming.
2. When you have made the 7th beat of the strumming on the Em chord (dead note), lift fingers of your left hand from the strings.
3. On the 8th beat of the strumming, play the open strings.
4. After hitting the open strings on the 8th beat, begin to place a G chord so that by the time the new round is played on the 1st beat, you already have a G chord placed.
5. Play the strumming.
6. When you have made the 7th beat of the strumming on the G chord (dead note), lift the fingers of your left hand from the strings.
7. On the 8th beat of the strumming, play open strings.
8. After hitting the open strings on the 8th beat, begin to play an Em chord so that by the time the new round is played on the 1st beat, you already have an Em chord in place.
9. Repeat from **step 1**.

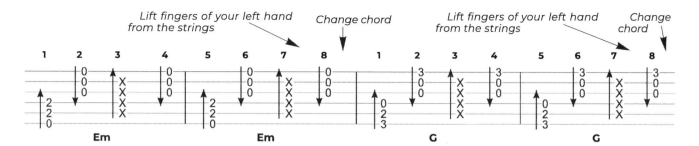

Your task is to play smoothly so that there are no jerks when you change chords. Your right hand will always play a rhythmic strumming pattern.

3.2. Ex.9

 3.3.

How to exclude (mute) the 6th string when playing strumming on chords from the 5th string (Am, A, C)

When playing strumming a chord from the 5th and 4th strings, it is important to exclude strings that are not part of the chord. If you leave the 6th string open, if you hit it, it will create a dissonant sound and the chord will sound strange and sometimes terribly nasty. In chords from the 5th string (Am, A, C), playing on the 6th string is excluded.

Mini exercise
The purpose of this simple exercise is to give you an understanding of the importance of muting strings that are not part of the chord and are dissonant. Make sure your guitar is in tune! If your guitar is out of tune, you won't be able to hear the difference between a correct and a dissonant sound.

1. Clamp the Dm chord.
2. With your right thumb, quickly swipe downward from the 4th string to the 1st string
3. Listen to the sound of the chord as it euphoniously sounds.
You can swipe the strings again and listen in.
4. On the same Dm chord, use your right thumb to quickly swipe down from the 6th string to the 1st string (i.e., across all strings).
5. Listen to how the sound became very strange and a mush of different sounds appeared. It sounds strange and horrible. This sound can be used as an artistic device, but do it consciously. For our purposes of beautiful playing, we should play clean chords.

How to eliminate the 6th string from playing
There are two ways to eliminate the 6th string and it is advisable to use them both at the same time!
1. Use the pad of your left thumb to touch the 6th string to muffle it. You may not have enough thumb length, which is fine if you are physiologically short. Or maybe you have a guitar that is too big and you need a smaller guitar.
2. Control your playing with your right hand and hit the strings aiming at the 5th string, excluding the 6th string from playing.

The goal in playing chords from the 5th string is to learn to hit only the 5th-4th-3rd strings with your right thumb.

At first, when you are still learning, look at the 6th string with your eyes and notice whether it vibrates or not. If it wobbles, it means you hit the 6th string and you should aim more accurately at the 5th string.

3.3. Exercise 10

Practicing hitting the 5th, 4th, 3rd strings with the thumb

Put an Am chord.
Important! For now, don't mute the 6th string with your left thumb and leave it open.

1. Strike downward with the right thumb on the 5th, 4th, 3rd strings
2. With rhythm and precision, repeat **step 1**.

The goal of the exercise is for you to learn how to hit the 5th string with your right thumb.

3.3. Exercise 11

Practicing strumming on the C chord with the 6th string muted

- Put an C chord.
- Touch the 6th string with your left thumb to mute it. With your right hand, pluck the 6th string and check that it is muted.
- Play a circular strumming pattern. Down - up - dead note - up (strike upward with the index finger in the same way, on the 1st, 2nd, 3rd strings).

Play for two minutes.

3.3. Exercise 12

Strumming on Am - C chords

It's the same as 3.2. exercise 9 (Playing strumming on the Em - G chord, **page 108**), only on Am - C chords.

1. Play an Am chord and mute the 6th string with your left thumb.
2. Start playing the strumming, aiming at the 5th string with your thumb as you strike down.
3. When you have made the 7th beat of the strumming on the Am chord (dead note), lift the fingers of your left hand off the strings.
4. On the 8th strumming beat, play the open strings.
5. After the open strings are struck on the 8th beat, begin to play a C chord so that by the time the new round is played on the 1st beat, you will have already played a C chord. When playing the C chord, muffle the 6th string with your thumb.
6. Play the strumming by aiming at the 5th string with your thumb when striking down.

7. When you make the 7th beat of the strumming on the C chord (dead note), lift the fingers of your left hand off the strings.

8. On the 8th beat of the strumming, play the open strings.

9. After hitting the open strings on the 8th beat, start playing an Am chord so that by the time the new round is played on the 1st beat, you have already played an Am chord and the 6th string is muted with your left thumb.

10. Repeat from **step 2**.

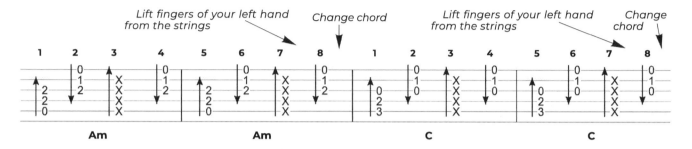

Do a checkup once in a while - Purposely take your left thumb off the 6th string and play the strumming. If the 6th string sounds, it means you need to control your right thumb more clearly and hit the 5th string. If the 6th string is muted, everything is fine.

3.3. Ex.12

 3.4

How to exclude the 6th and 5th strings when playing chords from the 4th string (D, Dm)

The 6th string has already been dealt with. It is muted with the left thumb and controlled by hitting the 5th string accurately with the right hand. The 5th string can also be muted with the thumb, if you have enough finger length. For example, I have enough finger length to muffle the 5th and 6th strings.

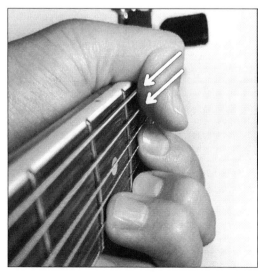
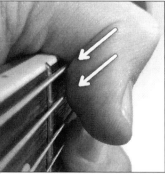

Put your thumb on top of the 6th and 5th strings so that it doesn't clamp them, but just touches them, muting the strings. Check that the strings are muted.

If the length of the left thumb is not enough, there is another way. You already know it - make a targeted strike with your right thumb on the 4th, 3rd, 2nd strings.

3.4. Exercise 13

Strumming a D chord

- Press the D chord.
- If your thumb is long enough, use it to strum the 6th and 5th strings. If you don't have enough length, just the 6th string.
- Play the strumming on the chord, aiming with your right thumb while striking down on the 4th,3rd,2nd (or 4th,3rd) strings (the upward stroke with your index finger is the same as always - on the 1st,2nd,3rd or 1st,2nd strings).

Play for two minutes.

3.4. Exercise 14

Strumming a Dm chord

- The same as the previous exercise, but with a Dm chord

Do a checkup once in a while - Purposely take your left thumb off the 6th (6th and 5th) string and play the strumming. If the 6th or 5th, or 6th and 5th strings sound, then you need to control your right thumb more clearly and start strumming from the 4th string. If the 6th and 5th strings are muted, everything is fine.

3.5

Practicing chord progressions and strumming

The following series of exercises are necessary for you:
1. Practiced chord progressions
2. Practiced transitions between chords
3. Practiced strumming
4. Better memorized chord placement
5. Created sound patterns for my brain of what chord progressions sound like (this will help me to easily pick up chords by ear for any song in the future)
6. Worked out the evenness of the rhythm.

Once you've mastered them you'll find it **VERY** easy to play any song. Use all the principles we've learned:
- Rules for playing chords from the 5th and 4th strings by muting strings that do not participate in the chord. (Chords from the 4th string D, Dm. Chords from the 5th string A, Am, C).
- Chord changes after the 8th beat of strumming on the open strings (3.2. STRUMMING. 4 - How to make chord changes when strumming, **page 108**).

In these exercises, play 2 strumming circles for each chord (down-and-up-snap-snap-snap-snap-snap-snap-snap-snap-snap-snap-snap and chord change).
In different exercises, you can play the strumming at different rhythm speeds to make it more varied and fun. For example, when practicing an exercise, you play the strumming a little faster. In another exercise, you play the fight a little slower, etc.

Be sure to practice all of the exercises below.
The criterion of practiced exercises is as follows - you have played at least 5 minutes of each exercise. The total should be 2 hours of total playing of exercises. This can be done in 2 days with 1 hour of play, in 4 days with 30 minutes of play, or in 6 days with 20 minutes of play.

Chords from the 6th and 5th strings:
3.5. Exercise 15. Strumming on Am - E chords
3.5. Exercise 16. Strumming on Am - G chords
3.5. Exercise 17. Strumming on E - A Chords

3.5. Exercise 18. Strumming on A - G chords
3.5. Exercise 19. Strumming on Em - C chords
3.5. Exercise 20. Strumming on C - G chords
3.5. Exercise 21. Strumming on E - G Chords

Chords from the 5th and 4th strings:
3.5. Exercise 22. Strumming on Am - Dm chords
3.5. Exercise 23. Strumming on Am - D chords
3.5. Exercise 24. Strumming on A - D chords

3.5. Exercise 25. Strumming on A - Dm chords
3.5. Exercise 26. Strumming on C - Dm chords
3.5. Exercise 27. Strumming on C - D chords

Chords from the 6th and 4th strings:
3.5. Exercise 28. Strumming on Em - Dm chords
3.5. Exercise 29. Strumming on Em - D chords
3.5. Exercise 30. Strumming on G - D chords

3.5. Exercise 31. Strumming on Dm - G chords
3.5. Exercise 31. Strumming on E - D chords
3.5. Exercise 31. Strumming on Dm - E chords

Exercises on chords from all strings (6th, 5th, 4th, strings)
3.5 Exercise 32. Strumming on G - C - G - D chords
3.5. Exercise 33. Strumming on G - C - A - D chords
3.5. Exercise 34. Strumming on A - D - A - E chords

3.5. Exercise 35. Strumming on Am - G - C - Em chords
3.5. Exercise 36. Strumming on Am - Dm - Am - E chords
3.5. Exercise 37. Strumming on Em - C - G - D chords

CHAPTER 4
MUSICAL RHYTHM

4.1

What is rhythm (feeling in time)

Understanding how rhythm works in music makes it possible to play any song, any musical part. And not only to play, but also to sing. A sense of rhythm allows us to understand music, to understand at what point in the music we need to extract the right sound. Understand how to count out the dimensions in music to play complex songs. Understanding rhythm is especially important if playing guitar solos, guitar riffs, melodies, or singing.

Going beyond playing guitar, a sense of rhythm allows us to feel the passage of time, to realize how much time has approximately passed. A sense of rhythm is very important in aerobic sports, such as long-distance running. In running, it is important to keep the same pace to maximize your energy and make it easy to run.

A sense of rhythm is important even when cutting vegetables with a knife. If you cut at a comfortable even pace, you can slice vegetables/fruit safely. And if you start making sudden jerks and sudden accelerations, you increase the risk of cutting yourself.

If you skip learning rhythm, it will be very difficult to play songs because you will get confused at what point where to make a chord change, especially in new songs that you don't know. It will be hard for you to understand and feel how to play more complex strumming and fingerpicking techniques.

Our whole lives are stitched with rhythms. Our walking, running and many other movements are rhythmic, our heartbeats are rhythmic, birdsong is rhythmic, bugs buzzing, waves hitting the shore, grasshoppers chirping, clock hands ticking, poems are also rhythmic compositions: "ta-tatata-tata-tatata-tata..." and many more. Even our speech has rhythm in it, so to one degree or another we all already understand something about rhythm.

The basic unit of rhythm is a repeated sound with equal intervals of time.
An example is the ticking of the second hand of a clock. It ticks at equal intervals of repetition. Between these equal intervals, there may be other sounds that will give a variety of rhythmic sounds.

Here's a prime example of what rhythm is in music and how important it is.
Be sure to listen to the audio examples I prepared. I made them on purpose with only one identical sound for the purity of the experiment. If you have heard these songs, you will immediately recognize them just by the rhythm alone. I tried to take very famous compositions.

Audio 4.1

How to feel the rhythm in your body

1. The rhythm we can hear is the ticking of the second hand.
2. To see the rhythmic movement of the second hand. By the way, the conductor of an orchestra controls the rhythm of the orchestra precisely due to the visual system by waving his hands.
3. To feel the vibrations of sound transmitted through the air (at high volume).

Lets focus specifically on the sense of rhythm in the body, because it is in the body that it is easiest to use when playing guitar. You've probably seen musicians stomping their feet, snapping their fingers, shaking their bodies, shaking their heads? They do it to be one with the music, with the rhythm. And it doesn't necessarily happen on purpose, but rather unconsciously. In essence, body swinging is a pendulum movement, which allows to keep the rhythmicity.

Everyone can feel the rhythm of the body differently. Shaking of the headstock, stomping of the foot, swinging of the arm, etc.

4.2 Exercise 1.a

Finding rhythm in the body

The goal of the exercise is to make you pay attention to which main body part you create the rhythm. It is the main part, because you can move your body in different ways and with different parts at the same time, but there will always be a leading part of your body, which you will use to track the rhythm.

It is better that you put a video of yourself in full height to see yourself from the side completely, because during the exercise you may not have enough attention to notice all the places in the body where you create swaying, and on the video you can easily trace it.

For the exercise you will need a device on which you can play your favorite song. (phone / phone + headphones / phone + speaker, computer, etc.). As a last resort, you can remember the song and listen to it in your imagination or even start humming it.

Instruction:
1. Set up a video recording device so you can be seen full-length
2. Stand / sit (as you feel comfortable).
3. Relax
4. Turn on your favorite piece of music (or any song you like)
5. Immerse yourself in the sensations in your body in relation to that song.

Listen to the music until you clearly feel that you have started to pump some part of your body. It can be headstock, leg, arm, fingers, torso tilts back and forth, left and right....

After the exercise, watch the video and pay attention to which / which body parts you were rocking.

4.2 Exercise 1.b

Rhythm in the body

Once you've found the place in your body that you're counting out the rhythm with, let's lock in that feeling.

Instruction:
1. Stand / sit (as you feel comfortable).
2. Relax
3. Start counting out loud evenly from 1 to 4, i.e. 1, 2, 3, 4, 1, 2, 3, 4, 1, 2, 3, 4, 1, 2, 3, 4... Each count at a rate of about 1 second
4. Along with counting, swing your active body part that you identified in the previous exercise for each count.

Count and wiggle a body part for 2-3 minutes to anchor the feeling in the body and the sense of rhythm.

4.3

How to count the rhythm and what it consists of

Let's talk about:
A. Tempo
B. Note durations
C. What is a musical bar
D. What is the measure of a bar

Tempo

The first unit of measurement of music is the tempo, or you can also call it the speed of the song. I'm sure you've heard your own heartbeat in different situations. When you are calm your heart beats slower, when you jog your heart will beat much faster. We measure heart rate by the number of beats per minute. It's the same thing in music. Tempo is measured in beats per minute. But beats per minute of "what" we'll talk about later.

4.3.B

Note durations

Understanding note durations will give you an understanding of the tempo we're measuring above, and by understanding note durations you'll be able to play different rhythmic patterns of strumming and fingerpicking in songs.

Note duration - is just a mathematical division of a note in multiples of 2. We can say half a glass of water and we know what that means. And it doesn't really matter what the volume or the size of the glass is. We just know it's half. A quarter of a glass of water. One-eighth of a glass of water (⅛). Also understandable. A whole apple, half an apple, a quarter of an apple, one-eighth of an apple... And so on with other objects..

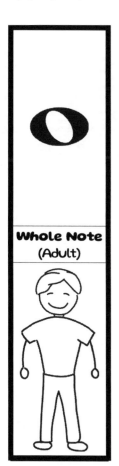

In music, the base duration of a note is a **whole note**, which makes sense. Let's look at it in comparison. Imagine an adult human being is like a whole note.

If you divide a whole note in half, you get 2 **half notes**. And if you divide the rise of an adult in half, you can conventionally say you get 2 children. 1 adults = 2 child.

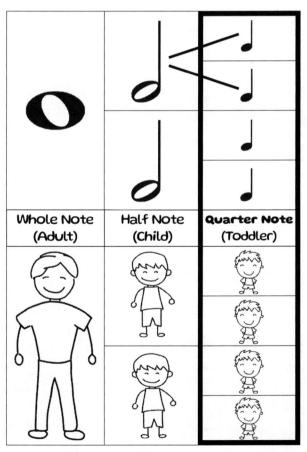

If you divide one half note in half, you get 2 quarter notes.

If you divide a child's height in half, you get 2 toddlers.

  1 adults = 2 child = 4 toddlers

  1 child = 2 toddlers

If a quarter note is divided in half you get 2 eighth notes.
If you divide the height of toddlers in half, you get 2 babies.

Whole Note (Adult)	Half Note (Child)	Quarter Note (Toddler)	Eighth Note (Baby)

In general, 8th notes like to be together in pairs (sometimes triples). That is, they seem to hold hands, so they are usually labeled together.
One eighth + one eighth form a pair (a pair is 2 eighths).

Then the 8th notes are divided in half again and 16 notes are obtained. From the name itself, it is logical that a sixteenth note means that there are 16 sixteenth notes in a whole note. Or there are 8 eighth notes in a whole note. Or there are four fourth notes in a whole note....

There are 32, 64 and even 128 notes, but they're rarely used. For now, we'll suffice with whole notes, half notes, fourth notes and eighth notes.

What is a musical bar

Rhythmic description of music relies on bar and bar size.

What a bar is?
1. Think of your favorite song or the first song that comes to your mind.
2. Visualize the horizontal audio track of that song as a time line. With the beginning of the song on the left and the end of the song on the right.

3. Picture the Empire State Building and rotate it so it is horizontal.

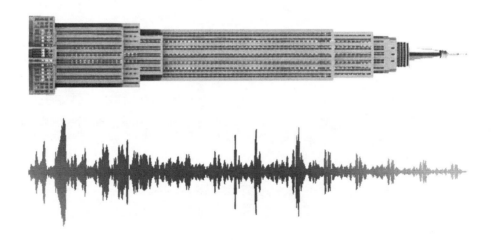

4. The height (duration) of the song = the height of the tower.
5. 1 floor of the tower = 1 bar of the song.

A bar is one piece of measurement in music, just like one floor in a building.
A bar in music is graphically indicated by a vertical line separating the musical ruler, and within the bar itself the notes are already written down.

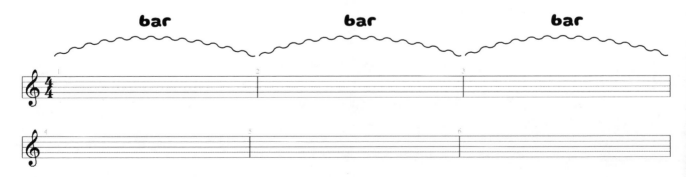

4.3.D

What is the measure of a bar

The size of the beat will determine our subjective perception of the music.

You've probably seen that height of one floor comes in different heights. There are 8 feet, 10 feet, 16 feet, 20 feet and others. It all depends on the building and its purpose. So, just as a floor comes in different heights, a beat comes in different sizes.

The size of a tact is written in two digits.
For example, let's take one of the most common measure sizes in music - four quarters. (the size of a beat is 4/4). This means that one beat is measured in 4 quarter notes.

4
4

To understand what 4/4 is let's imagine we were given the task of measuring the height of one floor of the Empire State Building. Imagine that we can choose exactly what to measure the height of the floor with, we can measure the height any way we want. We can measure the number of glasses, pencils, chairs between the floor and the ceiling, we can measure it in inches, we can measure it in human height. Let's measure by human height for the sake of example, because I gave the example of dividing notes with "human height division".

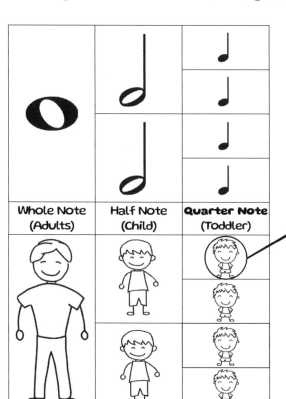

A bar is usually measured in quarter or eighth notes (less often in half or sixteenth notes). We are measuring in 4/4 and in our example with the height of a man it will be:
toddler (quarter note).

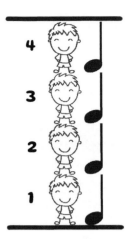

A bar is usually measured in quarter or eighth notes (less often in half or sixteenth notes). We are measuring in 4/4 and in our example with the height of a man it will be toddler (quarter note).

What we will measure with (glasses, pencils, chairs, inches, human height...) will conventionally define our frame of reference. Let's measure one floor of a tower in toddler (i.e., how much toddler will fit vertically from floor to ceiling). Let's assume that the tower builders are perfectionists and always make even numbers. And they put the height of 4 toddler in the floor height. We measured the height of the floor and it turns out that 4 toddlers fit from floor to ceiling.

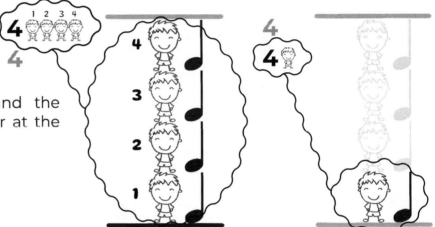

If we write down our scores as a fraction, with the thing we measured with (quarter note, i.e. toddler) at the bottom and the number of them in one bar at the top, we get this.

4
4

In reality (musical notation) it looks like this. It is written the same way we write and read text, from left to right.

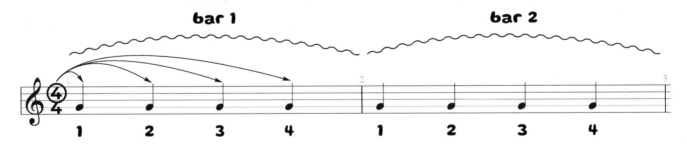

In music, there are very strong accents - these are the places from which the brain starts a reference point. In a bar, the strongest accent is the first note. Look at the picture - we have toddlers standing on top of each other. The first toddler is standing on the floor, he's very firmly on the floor. And all the other toddlers are on top of each other. If you remove the first toddler, the others will fall down. That's why the first toddler, i.e. the first note in a bar, is the strongest accent for perception.

4.3. Exercise 2

Size 4/4. Counting with quarter notes

This and the following exercises will give you an understanding of what a bar is, as well as improve your sense of rhythm.

In this exercise you will understand what tempo is in music. Read again the short description **4.3.A. - Tempo (page 116)**, and come back here.

You will need a watch with a second hand for the exercises! Preferably a mechanical watch. If you don't have a mechanical watch, you can use an app on your phone, but it is important that the app has a dial and a second hand that ticks and this tick can be heard. **The prerequisite for the exercise is the presence of a second hand and the sound of the second hand ticking in sync with the movement of the hand!**

Why do we use watches? There are 60 seconds in 1 minute, and 1 second is the rhythm that is biologically most comfortable for us, because at rest our heart beats an average of 60 beats per minute, i.e. every second. The average walking pace is about 60 steps per minute.

In this exercise, we're getting a pace of 60 beats per minute. And since we are now using 4/4, where each tick of a second is a quarter note, we have 60 beats per minute in quarter notes.

Task:

1. Place a clock next to you in front of you up to 1 meter away so you can hear ticking sound.
2. Remember exercise **4.2. Exercise 1 (a, b).** Finding rhythm in the body (**page 115**), I hope you found the leading part of your body to sway to the rhythm. (if you haven't, you can just bob your headstock back and forth for each count). If you have, use that part of your body to sway to each count.
3. While looking at the second hand, start counting out loud each tick of the second hand from 1 to 4x and simultaneously shake your body part to the bar. One, two, three, four. One, two, three, four. One, two, three, four...and so on.

Task - count in sync with the second.

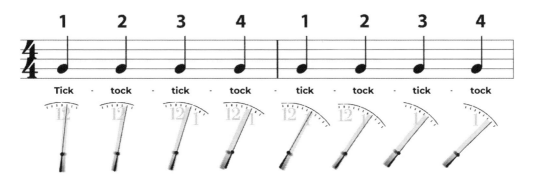

Counting from 1 to 4x will be 1 bar. When you start counting back to 1 after 4x, that's a new bar..

Criterion of the completed exercise - you synchronously count every tick of the arrow for at least 15 seconds straight..

Audio 4.3.Ex.2

- Incorrect example (does not hit)
- Correct example (even score)

That's a 4/4 bar. You counted 4 quarter notes in one bar. You can also count 2 half notes in that bar (1 half note = 2 quarter notes). Or even just one whole note. Next, practice counting with half notes and whole notes.

4.3. Exercise 3

Size 4/4. Counting with half notes

If in the last exercise you counted in 4 notes, now let's count the bar in half notes. Let me remind you that one half note = 2 fourth notes.

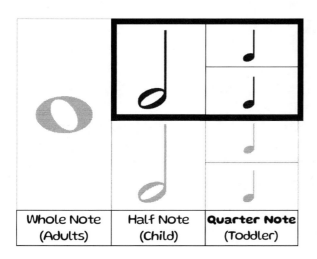

| Whole Note (Adults) | Half Note (Child) | Quarter Note (Toddler) |

Now you will count not in fourth notes, but in half notes, skipping one tick of the hand.

Place a clock in front of you (as in the previous exercise).

You need to count through one tick of the second hand. We have a bar size of 4/4 now, and 1 tick of the second hand is one fourth note. So if we count in one tick, we only get two counts.

Also swing the leading part of the body to synchronize with the rhythm.
Swing your body for each tick of the second hand, and say it out loud through the ticking:

Clock hand		Count
1.	Tick	-	**ONE** (body swing)
2.	Tock	-	*skip* (body swing)
3.	Tick	-	**TWO** (body swing)
4.	Tock	-	*skip* (body swing)

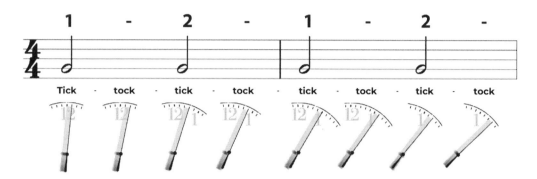

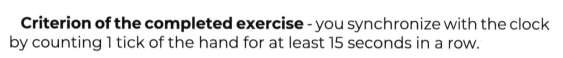

Audio 4.3.Ex.3

- Incorrect example (does not hit)
- Correct example (even score)

Criterion of the completed exercise - you synchronize with the clock by counting 1 tick of the hand for at least 15 seconds in a row.

4.3. Exercise 4

Size 4/4. Counting with a whole note

Everything is the same as in the previous exercises (including swinging the body every tick), only now the counting goes only on the first tick, on the count of one. Let me remind you that the bar size is now 4/4. A whole note consists of 4 quarter notes, that's why we will count only on the first tick every 4 seconds.

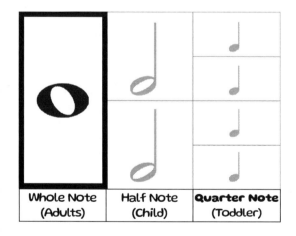

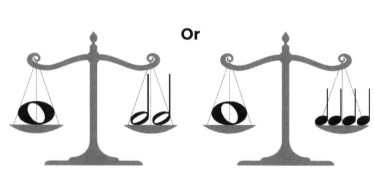

If you have trouble realizing that 4 seconds have passed, you can count 2,3,4 in your imagination or, for example, curl your fingers on your hand.

Clock hand		Count
1. Tick	-	**ONE** (body swing)
2. Tock	-	*skip* (body swing) / (if necessary, say "two" in imagination)
3. Tick	-	*skip* (body swing) / (if necessary, say "three" in imagination)
4. Tock	-	*skip* (body swing) / (if necessary, say "four" in imagination)

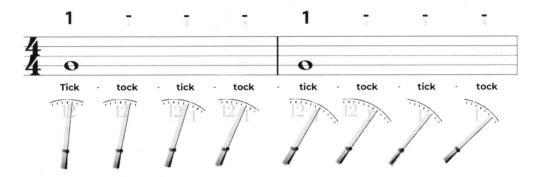

Audio 4.3.Ex.4

- Incorrect example (does not hit)
- Correct example (even score)

Criterion of the completed exercise - you synchronize with the clock to say the count of 1 tick every 4 seconds for at least 30 seconds in a row.

4.3. Exercise 5

Size 4/4. Counting with eighth notes

That's great! You've counted whole, half and fourth notes. Now let's figure out what the eighth notes are. In one fourth note, we have two eighth notes.

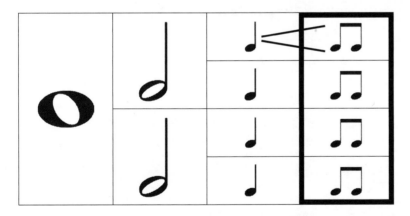

The bar size is 4/4, i.e. 4 quarter notes. One quarter note contains 2 eighth notes, a bar contains 4 quarter notes, so multiply 4 quarter notes by 2 and you get 8 eighth notes in a bar.

The second hand ticks the quarter notes. Your task is to count each tick and add a count between ticks of the second hand.
Between the counting add and.

Clock hand		Count
1. Tick	-	**ONE** (body swing)
2.	-	*and*
3. Tock	-	**TWO** (body swing)
4.	-	*and*
5. Tick	-	**THREE** (body swing)
6.	-	*and*
7. Tock	-	**FOUR** (body swing)
8.	-	*and*

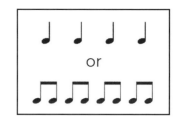

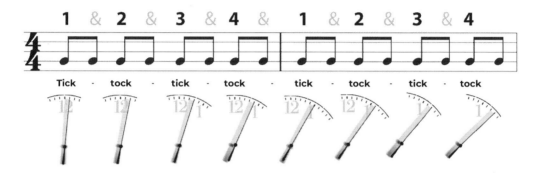

Audio 4.3.Ex.5

- Incorrect example (does not hit)
- Correct example (even score)

Criterion of the completed exercise - you synchronize with the clock to say the count for each tick and between ticks.

4.3. Exercise 6

Size 3/4. Counting with quarter notes

Another common size is **3/4** (there are 3 quarter notes in 1 bar).

It's the same thing you did with the clock, except now you count to 3 instead of 4.

So there are 3 quarter notes in 1 bar.

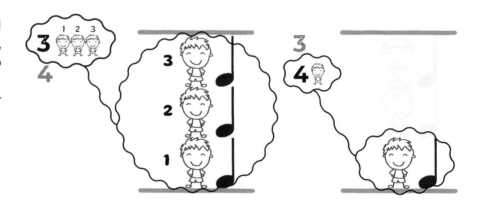

Remind yourself to sway your body (for unity with the rhythm).
Count for each tick of the second hand from 1 to 3.

Clock hand   Count

1. Tick   -   **ONE** (body swing)
2. Tock   -   **TWO** (body swing)
3. Tick   -   **THREE** (body swing)

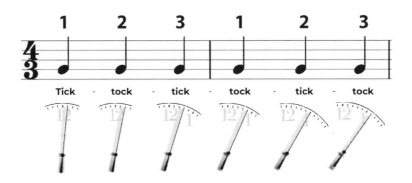

- Incorrect example (does not hit)
- Correct example (even score)

Criterion of the completed exercise - you synchronize with the clock and count every tick of the hand from 1 to 3 for at least 30 seconds in a row.

4.3. Exercise 7

Size 6/8. Counting with eighth notes

Another very popular bar size in music is **6/8**.

You know that different buildings may have different floor heights and we can measure the size of a floor (bar) not with 4 notes, but with 8 (baby). For example, let's imagine that unlike the builders of the Empire State Building in the Burj Khalifa Tower in Dubai made the height of the floor of a different size.Let's assume that the builders of the Burj Khalifa measured the height of baby floors and they had the height of one floor as 6 babies, i.e. 6/8.

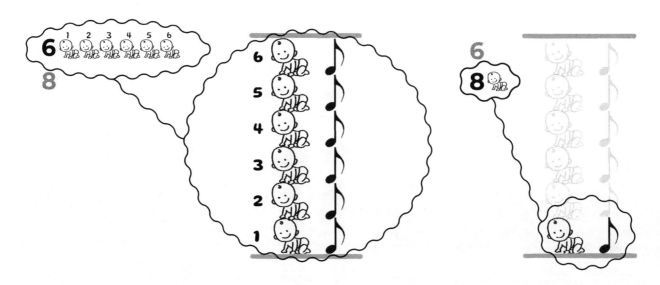

Regardless of the size of the bar, the first note of the bar will always be the strongest note for our perception. It is the one that will hold all the other notes in the bar together.

Count for each tick of the second hand from 1 to 6.

In 6/8, the eighth notes are not paired together, but in triplets, because 6/8 is a triplet measure.

Clock hand		Count
1. Tick	-	**ONE** (body swing)
2. Tock	-	**TWO** (body swing)
3. Tick	-	**THREE** (body swing)
4. Tock	-	**FOUR** (body swing)
5. Tick	-	**FIVE** (body swing)
6. Tock	-	**SIX** (body swing)

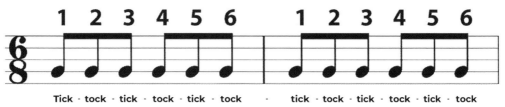

- Incorrect example (does not hit)
- Correct example (even score)

Audio 4.3.Ex.7

Criterion of the completed exercise - you synchronize with the clock and count every tick of the hand from 1 to 6 for at least 30 seconds in a row.

4.3. Exercise 8

Size 6/8. Counting with eighth notes

Now you will feel the difference in the pulsation of the rhythm. In this exercise you have to do 3 counts in 1 second.

Clock hand		Count
1. Tick	-	**ONE** (body swing)
2.	-	**two**
3.	-	**three**
4. Tock	-	**FOUR** (body swing)
5.	-	**five**
6.	-	**six**

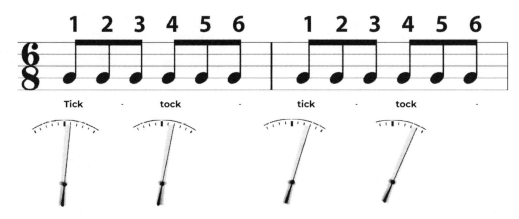

Audio 4.3.Ex.8

- Incorrect example (does not hit)
- Correct example (even score)

Criterion of the completed exercise - every second you say the three-digit count evenly over 30 consecutive seconds.

4.4

MUSIC SQUARE

Most music has a square-shaped structure. You already know what a bar is. Let's use the shape of a square as an example. A square has 4 sides. 1 side of a square is like 1 bar. There are 4 bars in one musical square.

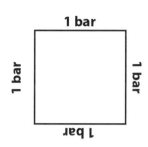

Listen to an example of a square in 6/8 size. There are 2 squares in this audio. You will immediately recognize where the 1st square ends and the 2nd square begins.

Audio 4.4

4.4 Example 1

The musical square is comfortable to our ears. For example, a chorus or verse in songs usually consists of 2 or 4 squares.

We understand music only because we have an inner sense of rhythm, i.e. we imagine how it should be and check the inner idea with reality, and this applies not only to the rhythmic part of music, but also to the frequency of sounds. I.e. we imagine what note should sound next and what rhythm (according to our idea) should be next.

I made an example where I broke the rhythm on purpose (i.e. I didn't complete the 2nd square) and also changed the melody.

Example 1

1. Pay attention to your body sensations after listening. Most likely you will feel that rhythmically the piece remains open and you want to complete it.

This happens because the music moves in a square. We hear the first square perfectly well, and the brain starts counting further, assuming that there will be a square again, but in the middle of the 2nd square everything breaks off. This gives us the feeling of a break, that something is not right at all.

2. Also pay attention to the melody. Since this song is very famous and you (I'm sure) have heard it, you already have an idea of what should sound next, but at the point where the melody changes abruptly your inner idea breaks down and it gives you a strange feeling.

4.4 Example 2

Listen to your imagination

Example 2

Let's take another song.

I want you to listen to your imagination (what you imagine) as you listen to the audio example. Pay attention in your imagination, when there is silence in the audio example, what do you hear?

If you listen carefully to what's in your headstock, you'll hear a continuation of that song. That is our inner imagination.

ABSTRACTS

If the rhythmic grid of a piece of music coincides with our inner sense of rhythm, then we fully understand the musical composition. If the rhythmic grid of the song differs from our inner sense of rhythm, we feel that something is wrong. The more coincidences, the more we understand the music. The less coincidence, the harder it is for us to understand the music.

By the way, all pop music is built on the expectation of our perceptions. That's why famous hits stay in our headstock for so long. Why does complex jazz seem like nonsense to an untrained listener? Because jazz has complex rhythmic sizes of bars, they are constantly changing, the melody is constantly changing and if the listener has no internal idea of what should happen next, no templates of such rhythmic grids and melodic transitions, then such music seems like complete chaos and nonsense to him.

CHAPTER 5
SONGS

An important preface to chapter 5

Here we come to the play of songs.

If for some reason you decide to skip all the tutorial chapters (Chapter 2, Chapter 3, Chapter 4) and start learning right from the songs, then provided you don't know how to play guitar with 100% probability you will fail. Your fingers will just physically refuse to get in the right place on the guitar, you will be putting one chord for several minutes, and it should be done in a fraction of seconds on automatic. Without the knowledge of rhythm that I described in Chapter 4, playing songs will be very difficult, especially if it's the first time you've heard them. So if you decide to play songs right away without learning, you are 100% responsible for the outcome (whatever it may be).

- The chords in the original songs are quite complicated for beginners. Therefore, we have simplified the chords and changed the tones of some songs to make them easier for you to play.

Changing the tonality of a song is like moving from one floor of a skyscraper to another floor in the same apartment. For example, we moved from the 90th floor to the 5th floor because the elevator is broken. It's still hard for you to walk up to the 90th floor, but you're used to walking and can easily get to the 5th floor. We will talk in detail about tones, what they are, how to change them and how to apply them in another book.

Files and video examples of how to play the songs in this book

For each song, I made:

- Audio files for examples so that you can listen to it and play it again.
- A special file in the program where you can listen to the song online, how it is played, and see the tablature for the song.
- Video example of how to play this song.

If you don't know a song, find it on YouTube or any search engine and listen to it.

How to play any songs?

To get you comfortable playing ANY song you need to take a few steps.

1. Listen to the original song and determine its size.
The size of the song may be listed in the source in which you watch the song (sometimes an erroneous size may be listed, so it can be checked).
How to determine the size:
- Turn on the song and start to pick up the rhythm with your body. Usually when we listen to music we like we automatically start swaying to the beat.
- Recall the feeling of perception when you did the clock exercise and counted the first number (one) - that was the strong accent. Feel (identify) the strong accent in the song, i.e., the beginning of each beat.
- Do you remember counting, for example, from 1 to 4 in 4/4 size? There was a strong accent on the number 1. Count the number of beats from one strong lobe to the next. The number of beats will be the measure.

2. Determine which way to play the song.
Any song can be played in different ways, which will give a different perception of the song (you can play strumming, fingerpicking, and other variations of these two playing techniques). The simplest way is to play a chord and to play it with the right thumb on the strings from top to bottom (further we will practice this method of playing). I.e. play a chord with a duration of the whole measure.
The nuance of this method (to play a whole note for the whole beat) - you need to count the rhythm in your imagination, count the numbers, stomp your foot, shake your body or any part of your body, or turn on the metronome. You can also visualize the melody of the song in your imagination and track the rhythm that way, or if you can sing, you can hum the melody / or sing the words.

We're already past fingerpicking strings and strumming. Strumming has the simplest variation, which is just a thumb swipe across the strings. Let's practice this technique, it's very simple. You'll probably be able to do it the 1st time, because you've

Playlist link to all videos (exercises, examples, songs, etc.)

youtube.com/playlist?list=PLD9E7uLFX4pyHo5C8x1wUhMBEkJW73wiL

5.3 Exercise 1

Guiding the thumb of the right hand over the strings from top to bottom

1. Put down any chord, such as **Em**
2. Put your right hand in the strumming position
3. Start counting out loud evenly from 1 to 4x, and every 1st count, use your right thumb to stroke the strings from 6 to 1.

```
   1   -   2   -   3   -   4   -   1   -   2   -   3   -   4   -
   0                               0
   0                               0
   0                               0
   2                               2
   2                               2
   0                               0
```

Play for two minutes.

5.3.Ex.1

 5.3 Exercise 2

The same as the previous exercise, except that you do the strings on every 2nd count. i.e. on count 1 and count 3.

```
   1   -   2   -   3   -   4   -   1   -   2   -   3   -   4   -
   0               0               0               0
   0               0               0               0
   0               0               0               0
   2               2               2               2
   2               2               2               2
   0               0               0               0
```

Play for two minutes.

5.3.Ex.2

ALOUETTE

This song is in the size of **4/4**. The tempo is **120** (i.e. if you turn the metronome on at 120 beats per minute, each beat will be 1/4. 4 beats of the metronome would equal 1 bar. P.S. you don't have to use a metronome (you may or may not use a metronome, whatever you want. Try it both ways).

This song is best played by simply running your thumb from bottom to top of the strings, on the 1st and 3rd counts (as *5.3. exercise 2* **page 135**).

Lyrics

Alouette, gentille alouette,
Alouette, je te plumerai.

Je te plumerai la tête,
Je te plumerai la tête,
Et la tête, et la tête,
Alouette, alouette...

Alouette, gentille alouette,
Alouette, je te plumerai.

CHORDS

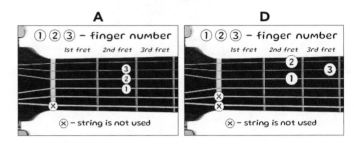

1	2	**3**	4	**1**	2	**3**	4
A	- lo - ue	- tte,		gen-tille alo	- uet	- te	

```
--------------------------------------------------
---2------------2------------0------------2--------
---3------------3------------2------------3--------
---2------------2------------2------------2--------
---0------------0------------2------------0--------
--------------------------|--0---------------------
```

Score	**1** - 2 - 3 - 4 -	**1** - 2 - 3 - 4 -
Chords	**D** **D**	**A** **D**
Lyrics	A - lou - et - te,	gen-tille alou - ette,

1 - 2 - 3 - 4 -   **1** - 2 - 3 - 4 -
D   **D**   **A**   **D**
A   -   lou - et   -   te,   gen-tille alou - ette,

1 - 2 - 3 - 4 -   **1** - 2 - 3 - 4 -
D   **D**   **A**   **D**
A   -   lou - et   -   te,   je   te   plume - rai.

1 - 2 - 3 - 4 -   **1** - 2 - 3 - 4 -
D   **D**   **A**   **D**
A   -   lou - et   -   te,   gen-tille alou - ette,

1 - 2 - 3 - 4 -   **1** - 2 - 3 - 4 -
D   **D**   **A**   **D**
A   -   lou - et   -   te,   je   te   plume - rai.

1 - 2 - 3 - 4 -   **1** - 2 - 3 - 4 -
D   **D**   **A**   **D**
Je   te   plume - rai   la   tête,   Je   te   plume - rai   la   tête,

1 - 2 - 3 - 4 -   **1** - 2 - 3 - 4 -
A   **A**   **A**   **A**
Et   la   tête,   et   la   tête,   alouette,   alouette...

1 - 2 - 3 - 4 -   **1** - 2 - 3 - 4 -
D   **D**   **A**   **D**
A   -   lou - et   -   te,   gen-tille alou - ette,

1 - 2 - 3 - 4 -   **1** - 2 - 3 - 4 -
D   **D**   **A**   **D**
A   -   lou - et   -   te,   je   te   plume - rai.

ALPHABET SONG

Size **4/4**. Tempo **100**.
This song is best played by simply sliding your thumb down the strings, on the 1st and 3rd counts.

Lyrics
A - B - C - D - E - F - G
H - I - J - K - L - M - N - O - P
Q - R - S - T - U and V
W - X - Y and Z
Now I know my A - B - C's
Next time won't you sing with me?

CHORDS

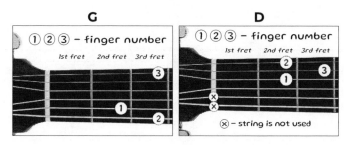

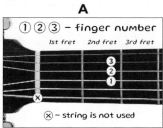

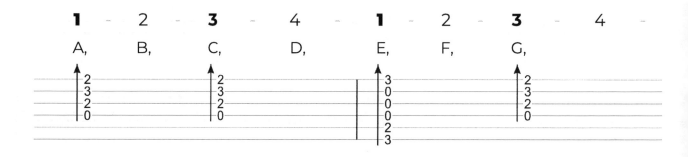

	1	-	2	-	3	-	4	-	**1**	-	2	-	3	-	4	-
Score	**1**	-	2	-	3	-	4	-	**1**	-	2	-	3	-	4	-
Chords	D				D				A				D			
Lyrics	A,		B,		C,		D,		E,		F,		G,			

1	-	2	-	3	-	4	-	**1**	-	2	-	3	-	4	-
D				D				G				D			
A,		B,		C,		D,		E,		F,		G,			

1	-	2	-	3	-	4	-	**1**	-	2	-	3	-	4	-
G				D				A				D			
H,		I,		G,		K,		L,	M,	N,	O,	P			

1	-	2	-	3	-	4	-	**1**	-	2	-	3	-	4	-
D				G				D				A			
Q,		R,		S,				T,		U,		V,			

1	-	2	-	3	-	4	-	**1**	-	2	-	3	-	4	-
D				G				D				A			
W,				X,				Y		and		Z.			

1	-	2	-	3	-	4	-	**1**	-	2	-	3	-	4	-
D				D				G				D			
Now		I		know		my		A,		B,		C's			

1	-	2	-	3	-	4	-	**1**	-	2	-	3	-	4	-
G				D				A				D			
Next		time		won't		you		sing		with		me?			

AMAZING GRACE

Size **3/4**. Tempo **110**. (i.e. if you turn the metronome on at 110 beats per minute, each beat will be 1/4. 3 beats of the metronome will equal 1 bar.

This song is best played by simply sliding your thumb down the strings. The duration of 1 chord will be 3 beats of the metronome. Slide your thumb down the strings on the 1st count.

Lyrics

Amazing Grace, how sweet the sound
That saved a wretch like me
I once was lost but now am found
Was blind, but now I see.

CHORDS

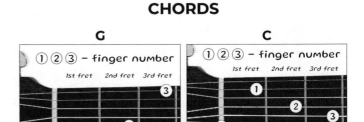

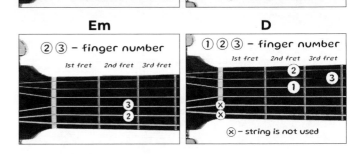

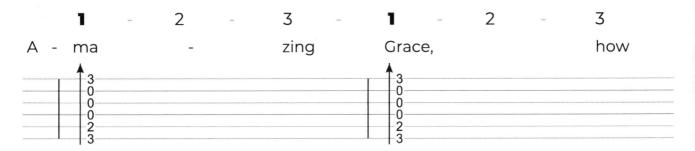

Score	**1**	-	2	-	3	-	**1**	-	2	-	3	-
Chords	G						G					
Lyrics	A - ma		-		zing		Grace,				how	

1	-	2	-	3	-	**1**	-	2	-	3	-
G						G					
A - ma		-		zing		Grace,				how	

1	-	2	-	3	-	**1**	-	2	-	3	-
C						G					
sweet				the		sound				that	

1	-	2	-	3	-	**1**	-	2	-	3	-
Em						C					
saved				a		wretch				like	

1	-	2	-	3	-	**1**	-	2	-	3	-
D						D					
me.										I	

1	-	2	-	3	-	**1**	-	2	-	3	-
G						G					
once				was		lost				but	

1	-	2	-	3	-	**1**	-	2	-	3	-
C						G					
now				am		found				was	

1	-	2	-	3	-	**1**	-	2	-	3	-
Em						C					
blind,				but		now				I	

1	-	2	-	3	-	**1**	-	2	-	3	-
G						G					
see.											

ALL THROUGH THE NIGHT

This song is in **4/4** size and tempo **120** (i.e. if you turn the metronome on at 120 beats per minute, each beat will be 1/4. 4 beats of the metronome will equal 1 bar.

This song can be played in many ways:
1. Swipe down the strings with the thumb on the 1st and 3rd counts
2. Play fingerpicking on the strings.

If you play fingerpicking, then fingerpicking will be 8 notes, i.e. you pull 2 strings for 1 count. (1 and 2 and 3 and 4 and). To learn which strings to play, see either the video, or the additional file in the link, or Chapter 2 - BASIC Fingerpicking Pattern (**page 95**).

Lyrics
Sleep my child and peace attend thee
All through the night
Guardian angels God will send thee
All through the night

Soft the drowsy hours are creeping
Hill and vale in slumber sleeping
I my loving vigil keeping
All through the night

1. Thumb swipe down the strings on the 1st and 3rd counts:

1	2	**3**	4	**1**	2	**3**	4
Sleep		my child	and	peace		at - tend	thee

```
|2-------  |3-------  |0-------  |0-------
|3-------  |0-------  |0-------  |2-------
|2-------  |0-------  |1-------  |2-------
|0-------  |0-------  |2-------  |2-------
          |2-------  |2-------  |0-------
          |3-------  |0-------
```

2. By fingerpicking:

1	2	**3**	4	**1**	2	**3**	4
Sleep		my child	and	peace		at - tend	thee

```
--------------------2---------------------------------------------------------2----
------------3---------------------0-----------------------0-----------------2-------
--------2-----------------0-----------------1-------------------------2-------------
0-----------------------------0---------2------------------------2------------------
                                                     0
------------3-------------------------------0--------------------------------------
```

1	-	2	-	3	-	4	-	**1**	-	2	-	3	-	4	-
D				**G**				**E**				**A**			
Sleep		my	child	and		peace		at - tend		thee					

1	-	2	-	3	-	4	-	**1**	-	2	-	3	-	4	-
G				**A**				**D**				**D**			
All			through		the night.										

1	-	2	-	3	-	4	-	**1**	-	2	-	3	-	4	-
D				**G**				**E**				**A**			
Guar	-	dian	an	-	gels	God			will send		thee				

1	-	2	-	3	-	4	-	**1**	-	2	-	3	-	4	-
G				**A**				**D**				**D**			
All			through		the night.										

1	-	2	-	3	-	4	-	**1**	-	2	-	3	-	4	-
G				**G**				**G**				**G**			
Soft	the		drow - sy			hours	are		cre	-	eping				

1	-	2	-	3	-	4	-	**1**	-	2	-	3	-	4	-
Em				**Em**				**G**				**A**			
Hill	and		vale	in		slum	-		ber sle	-	eping				

1	-	2	-	3	-	4	-	**1**	-	2	-	3	-	4	-
D				**G**				**E**				**A**			
I		my lo	-	ving		vi	-		gil ke	-	eping				

1	-	2	-	3	-	4	-	**1**	-	2	-	3	-	4	-
G				**A**				**D**				**D**			
All			through		the night.										

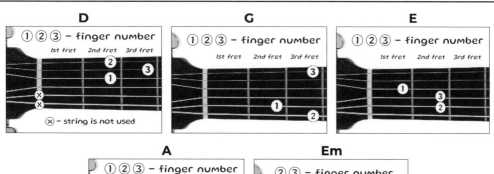

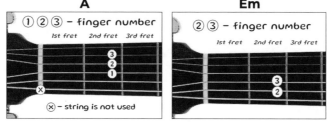

5.4

Gallop Strumming

There are different variations of the strumming game. This variation is very cool and creates the effect of riding a horse.

There are 2 ways to play with the thumb:
1. Thumb strikes 2nd-3rd bass strings (as in normal strumming)
2. Thumb strikes only the first bass string of the chord (the thickest string in the chord). In chords from the 6th string it is the 6th string, in chords from the 5th string it is the 5th string, in chords from the 4th string it is the 4th string.

- The index finger plays the bottom 3 strings with a downstroke, then an upstroke.

5.4 Exercise 1

Exercise place any chord and play this strumming pattern in two variations! Practice the 1st variation first, then the 2nd variation.

Variants:
1. When striking with your thumb, strike 2-3 bass strings. The index finger plays the bottom 3 strings with a downstroke, then an upstroke.
2. When striking with your thumb, pluck only one bass string. In chords from the 6th string it is the 6th string, in chords from the 5th string it is the 5th string, in chords from the 4th string it is the 4th string. The index finger plays the bottom 3 strings with a downstroke, then an upstroke.

Each punch is received for 1 count:
1. Thumb strikes the bass string downward (2-3 strings or one string)
2. Index finger strikes the lower strings upward
3. Index finger strikes the lower strings downward
4. Index finger strikes the lower strings upward

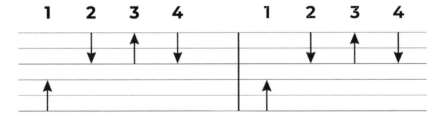

Play it for a couple minutes to get a feel for the movement.

5.4.Ex.1

5.4 Exercise 2

Now let's take out the one shot that was on the 2nd. So we skip that shot and play on 1st, 3rd, 4th.

(Work on option 1 first, then option 2)
1. When striking with your thumb, strike the 2nd-3rd bass strings with your thumb
2. When striking with your thumb, pluck only one bass string.

1. Thumb strikes the bass string downward (2nd-3rd strings or one string)
2. Skip
3. Index finger strikes the lower strings downward
4. Index finger strikes the lower strings upward.

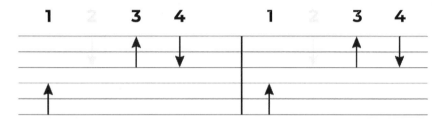

Play for a few minutes to get a feel for this rhythm. Then we will use this rhythm in the next song and some other songs.

5.4.Ex.2

BUFFALO GALS

I recommend reading it again (3.2. How to make chord changes when playing strumming on **page 108**).

Size **4/4**. Tempo **200**. (i.e. if you turn on the metronome at 200 beats per minute, each beat will be 1/4. 4 beats of the metronome will be equal to 1 bar).

It will be cool to play this song with the Gallop Strumming strumming that you practiced in the previous exercises. Play the strumming as in the previous exercise (*5.4 Exercise 2*).

Lyrics
As I was walking down the street
Down the street, down the street,
A little pretty gal I chanced to meet,
Oh she was fair to see.

Chorus
Buffalo Gals, won't you come out tonight,
Come out tonight, come out tonight.
Buffalo Gals, won't you come out tonight
And dance by the light of the moon.

CHORDS

A

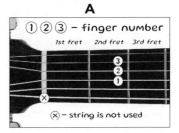

E

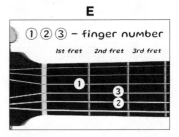

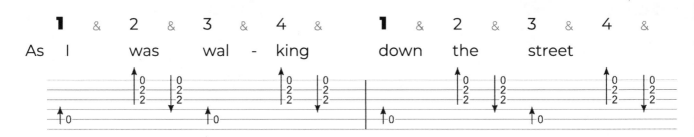

Video

Guitar Tabs

1	&	2	&	3	&	4	&	**1**	&	2	&	3	&	4	&
A								A							
As I		was		wal	-	king		down		the				street	

1	&	2	&	3	&	4	&	**1**	&	2	&	3	&	4	&
E								A							
Down		the		street,				down		the		street,		A	

1	&	2	&	3	&	4	&	**1**	&	2	&	3	&	4	&
A								A							
little		pretty		gal		I		chanced to				meet,		Oh	

1	&	2	&	3	&	4	&	**1**	&	2	&	3	&	4	&
E								A							
she		was		fair		to		see.							

1	&	2	&	3	&	4	&	**1**	&	2	&	3	&	4	&
A								A							
Buf	-	falo		Gals,		won't you come out				to - night,					

1	&	2	&	3	&	4	&	**1**	&	2	&	3	&	4	&
E								A							
Come out		to - night,						come out		to - night,					

1	&	2	&	3	&	4	&	**1**	&	2	&	3	&	4	&
A								A							
Buf	-	falo		Gals,		won't you come out				to - night,		and			

1	&	2	&	3	&	4	&	**1**	&	2	&	3	&	4	&
E								A							
dance		by		the light		of		the moon.							

BLOW THE MAN DOWN!

Size **3/4**. The tempo is **140**. (i.e. if you turn the metronome on at 140 beats per minute, each beat will be 1/4. 3 beats of the metronome will equal 1 bar.

This song can be played in many ways:
1. Sliding the thumb down the strings on the 1st count
2. Play a strumming gallop.

Lyrics
Come all you young fellows who follow the sea
Wey hey, blow the man down
And pray pay attention and listen to me
Gimme some time to blow the man down.

CHORDS

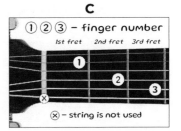

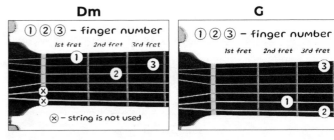

1. Variation of playing with the thumb on the strings:

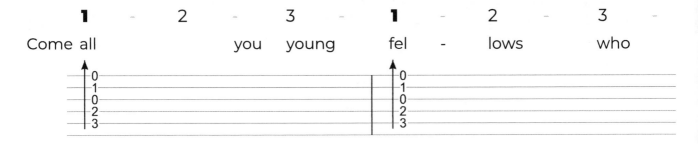

Come

1 C	-	2	-	3	-	**1** C	-	2	-	3	-
all				you	young	fel	-	lows		who	

1 C	-	2	-	3	-	**1** C	-	2	-	3	-
fol	-			low	the	sea					

1 C	-	2	-	3	-	**1** C	-	2	-	3	-
Wey						hey					

1 Dm	-	2	-	3	-	**1** G	-	2	-	3	-
blow				the	man	down				and	

1 Dm	-	2	-	3	-	**1** G	-	2	-	3	-
pray				pay	at	- ten	-	tion		and	

1 Dm	-	2	-	3	-	**1** G	-	2	-	3	-
lis	-	ten		to		me					

1 G	-	2	-	3	-	**1** G	-	2	-	3	-
Gim	-	me		some		time				to	

1 G	-	2	-	3	-	**1** C	-	2	-	3	-
blow				the	man	down.					

2. Variation of playing with the thumb on the strings (5.4. Ex.3):

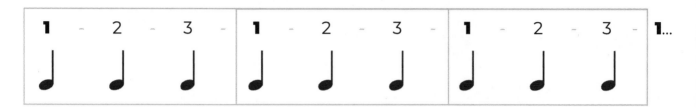

1. Start counting out loud from 1 to 3. You're counting quarter notes.

2. Add an "and" between the 2nd and 3rd counts. So you're counting the "2 and" as eighth notes.

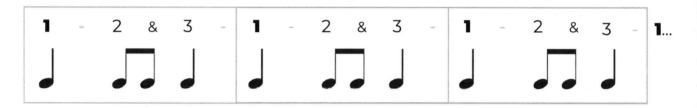

3. You counted 2 out loud, now skip counting 2 out loud and count 2 only in your imagination. I.e. now on the count of 2 you don't say anything out loud, but you keep silent. You get 1 - and 3 - . This will be our basic rhythm pattern.

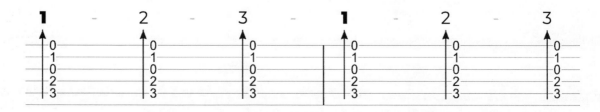

Play a C chord and do the same thing you did in the last exercise, but instead of counting, play strumming.

1. Start making a top-to-bottom sweep with your right thumb across all strings. On each count (1 - 2 - 3).

2. Add an "and" between the 2nd and 3rd counts and now on the "2, &, 3" counts play only the 2-3 strings of the chord with your index finger. Remember the basic rule of strumming? Thumb plays bass strings, index finger plays thinner strings.

- Now, on the count of 1, use your thumb to tap all the strings of the chord
- On the count of 2, strike down with your index finger on the thin strings
- On the count and strike upward with your index finger on the thin strings
- On the count of 3, strike down with your index finger on the thin strings.

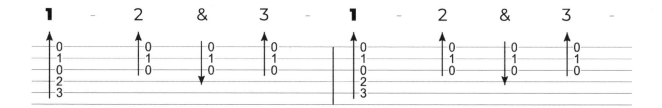

3. Eliminate playing on the count of 2. Now play only on "1, and, 3".

- On the count of 1, slide your thumb across all strings of the chord
- On the count of 2 skip
- On the count and strike upward with your index finger on the thin strings
- On the count of 3, strike down with your index finger on the thin strings.

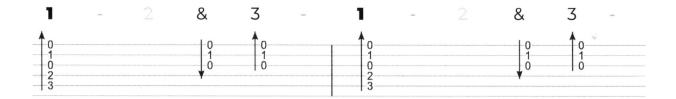

Play this strumming for 5-10 minutes to create a pattern in your brain for this type of strumming.

Then you can play the song "**Blow the Man Down!**" with this strumming pattern!

5.4 Ex.3

5.4 Ex.4

CHRISTMAS TREE

Size **3/4**. The tempo is **90**. (i.e. if you turn the metronome on at 90 beats per minute, each beat will be 1/4. 3 beats of the metronome will equal 1 bar.

This song can be played by simply running your thumb down the strings for every 1st count.

Lyrics
O Christmas tree, o Christmas tree
Thy leaves are so unchanging
O Christmas tree, o Christmas tree
Thy leaves are so unchanging
Not only green when summer's here
But also when it's cold and drear
O Christmas tree, o Christmas tree
Thy leaves are so unchanging

CHORDS

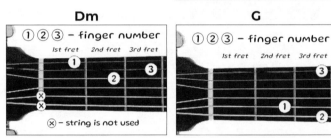

	1		2		3		**1**		2		3	
O	Christmas		tree,				o	Christmas		tree		thy

```
1  |--0--
   |--1--
   |--0--
   |--2--
   |--3--

1  |--0--
   |--1--
   |--0--
   |--2--
   |--3--
```

Video

Guitar Tabs

1	-	2	-	3	-	1	-	2	-	3	-
C						**C**					
O Christmas tree,						o Christmas tree					thy

1	-	2	-	3	-	1	-	2	-	3	-
Dm						**C**					
leaves are so		un	-	chang	-	ing.					O

1	-	2	-	3	-	1	-	2	-	3	-
C						**C**					
Christmas tree,						o Christmas tree					thy

1	-	2	-	3	-	1	-	2	-	3	-
Dm						**C**					
leaves are so		un	-	chang	-	ing.					Not

1	-	2	-	3	-	1	-	2	-	3	-
C						**Dm**					
only green				when	summer's	here,					but

1	-	2	-	3	-	1	-	2	-	3	-
G						**C**					
also when				it's	cold and	drear.					O

1	-	2	-	3	-	1	-	2	-	3	-
C						**C**					
Christmas tree,						o Christmas tree					thy

1	-	2	-	3	-	1	-	2	-	3	-
Dm						**C**					
leaves are so		un	-	chang	-	ing.					

GOD IS SO GOOD

This song is in **4/4** size and tempo **120** (i.e. if you turn the metronome on at 120 beats per minute, each beat will be 1/4. 4 beats of the metronome will equal 1 bar.

This song can be played in many ways:
1. Sliding your thumb down the strings, on the 1st count. In this variation it will be especially important either to imagine the melody, or to hum it, or to count 1-2-3-4, because rhythmically there are large distances between the chords and it is important to keep counting the rhythm.
2. Gallop strumming (any variation. The thumb plays only one string or plays several strings).
3. Fingerpicking.

Lyrics
God is so good,
God is so good,
God is so good,
He's so good to me.

1. Sliding the thumb down the strings, on the 1st count:

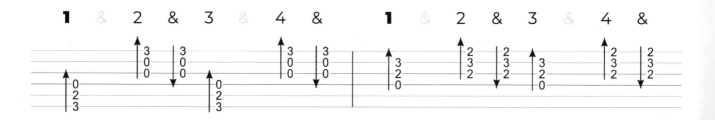

2. Strumming gallop:
If you play a strumming gallop, the pattern will be like this (we've already gone over it - **page 145**):

page 145

Rhythmic strikes on the strings will be on "1, 2, and, 3, 4, and "

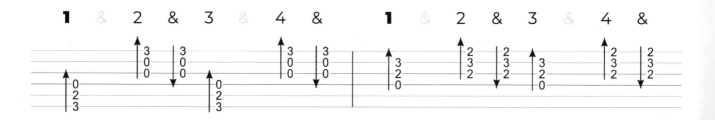

| Video | Guitar Tabs 1 | Guitar Tabs 2 | Guitar Tabs 3 |

3. String fingerpicking - use the string fingerpicking pattern (**page 95**).
1 count - 1 pluck of a string.

1	-	2	-	3	-	4	-	**1**	-	2	-	3	-	4
God				is		so		good,						

```
|--------------------------------2-|
|----------------0-----------3-----|
|----------0-------------2---------|
|------0-------------0-------------|
|3--------------------------------|
```

1	-	2	-	3	-	4	-	**1**	-	2	-	3	-	4	-
G								**D**							
God				is		so		good,							

1	-	2	-	3	-	4	-	**1**	-	2	-	3	-	4	-
D								**G**							
God				is		so		good,							

1	-	2	-	3	-	4	-	**1**	-	2	-	3	-	4	-
G								**C**							
God				is		so		good,				he's		so	

1	-	2	-	3	-	4	-	**1**	-	2	-	3	-	4	-
G				**D**				**G**							
Good				to				me.							

CHORDS

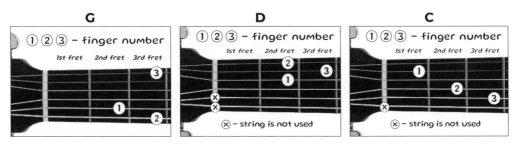

HAPPY BIRTHDAY

Size **3/4**. Tempo **120**. (i.e. if you turn on the metronome at 120 beats per minute, each beat will be 1/4. 3 beats of the metronome will equal 1 bar).

Lyrics
Happy Birthday to you,
Happy Birthday to you,
Happy Birthday dear (name),
Happy Birthday to you!

This song can be played by simply running your thumb down the strings on the 1st count.

1	2	3	**1**	2	3
Happy Birth - day	to	you,			

```
  3                    2
  0                    3
  0                    2
  0                    0
  2
  3
```

happy

1 **G**	-	2	-	3	-	**1** **D**	-	2	-	3	-
Birth	-	day		to		you,				happy	

1 **D**	-	2	-	3	-	**1** **G**	-	2	-	3	-
Birth	-	day		to		you,				happy	

1 **G**	-	2	-	3	-	**1** **C**	-	2	-	3	-
Birth	-	day		dear		(na	-	me),		happy	

1 **G**	-	2	-	3 **D**	-	**1** **G**	-	2	-	3	-
Birth	-	day		to		you.					

CHORDS

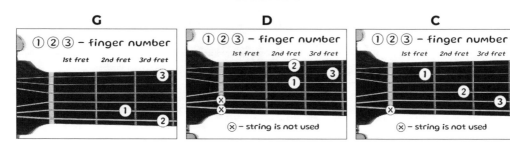

G   D   C

JINGLE BELLS

Size **4/4**. The tempo is **90**. (i.e. if you turn the metronome on at 90 beats per minute, each beat of the metronome will be 1/4. 4 beats of the metronome will be equal to 1 bar.

This song can be played in many ways:
1. Sliding the thumb down the strings on the 1st and 3rd counts (i.e. every 2nd count).
2. Play the strumming down - up - dead note - up (which you practiced in chapter 3).

Lyrics
Dashing through the snow
In a one-horse open sleigh
O'er the fields we go
Laughing all the way
Bells on bobtails ring
Making spirits bright
What fun it is to ride and sing
A sleighing song tonight

Chorus
Oh! Jingle bells, jingle bells
Jingle all the way
Oh, what fun it is to ride
In a one-horse open sleigh, hey
Jingle bells, jingle bells
Jingle all the way
Oh, what fun it is to ride
In a one-horse open sleigh

CHORDS

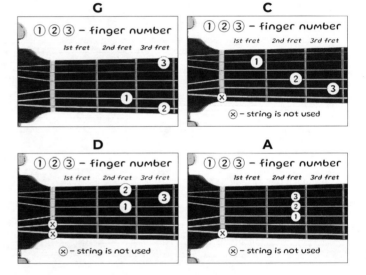

1. **Sliding the thumb down the strings on the 1st and 3rd counts (i.e. every 2nd count):**

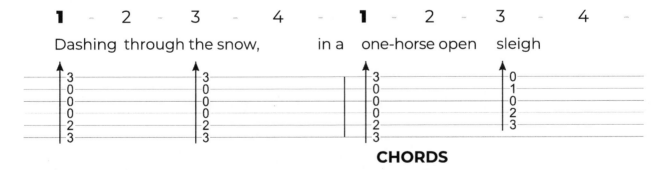

CHORDS

Video

Guitar Tabs 1

Guitar Tabs 2

2. Strumming (down - up - dead note - up):

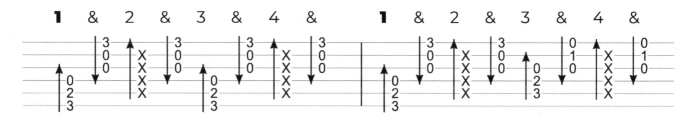

1	-	2	-	3	-	4	-	**1**	-	2	-	3	-	4	-
G				**G**				**G**				**C**			

Dashing through the snow,   in a one-horse open   sleigh

1	-	2	-	3	-	4	-	**1**	-	2	-	3	-	4	-
C				**D**				**D**				**G**			

O'er the fields we go   laughing all   the way

1	-	2	-	3	-	4	-	**1**	-	2	-	3	-	4	-
G				**G**				**G**				**C**			

Bells on bobtails ring.   Making   spirits   bright   what

1	-	2	-	3	-	4	-	**1**	-	2	-	3	-	4	-
C				**D**				**D**				**G**			

Fun it   is   to   ride and sing a   sleighing song to - night.   Oh!

1	-	2	-	3	-	4	-	**1**	-	2	-	3	-	4	-
G				**G**				**G**		**C**		**G**			

Jin - gle bells,   jin - gle bells.   Jin - gle   all   the way.

1	-	2	-	3	-	4	-	**1**	-	2	-	3	-	4	-
C				**G**				**A**				**D**			

Oh, what fun it   is   to   ride. In a one-horse o - pen sleigh,   hey

1	-	2	-	3	-	4	-	**1**	-	2	-	3	-	4	-
G				**G**				**G**		**C**		**G**			

Jin - gle bells,   jin - gle bells.   Jin - gle   all   the way.

1	-	2	-	3	-	4	-	**1**	-	2	-	3	-	4	-
C				**G**				**D**				**G**			

Oh, what fun it   is   to   ride. In a one-horse o - pen sleigh.

HUSH, LITTLE BABY

Size **4/4**. Tempo **100**. (i.e. if you turn the metronome on at 100 beats per minute, each beat will be 1/4. 4 beats of the metronome will equal 1 bar.

This song can be played in many ways:
1. Sliding the thumb down the strings on the 1st and 3rd counts (i.e. every 2nd count)
2. Play a strumming gallop
3. Play fingerpicking (1 count = 1 string plucking).

Lyrics
Hush, little baby, don't say a word,
Mama's gonna buy you a mockingbird.
And if that mockingbird don't sing,
Mama's gonna buy you a diamond ring.

And if that diamond ring turns brass,
Mama's gonna buy you a looking glass.
And if that looking glass is broke,
Mama's gonna buy you a billy goat,

And if that billy goat won't pull,
Mama's gonna buy you a cart and a bull.
And if that cart and bull turn over,
Mama's gonna buy you a dog named Rover.

And if that dog named Rover won't bark,
Mama's gonna buy you a horse and a cart.
And if that horse and cart fall down,
You'll still be the sweetest little baby in town.

So hush little baby, don't you cry.
Daddy loves you and so do I.

CHORDS

C

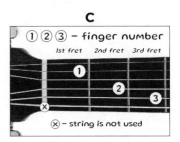

⊗ – string is not used

G

1. **Sliding your thumb down the strings on the 1st and 3rd counts (i.e. every 2nd count):**

| **1** | - | 2 | - | **3** | - | 4 | - | **1** | - | 2 | - | **3** | - | 4 | - |

Hush, lit - tle ba   -   by,   don't say a   word,

```
----|0------------|0------------|3------------|3------------
----|1------------|1------------|0------------|0------------
----|0------------|0------------|0------------|0------------
----|2------------|2------------|0------------|0------------
----|3------------|3------------|2------------|2------------
    |             |             |3            |3
```

Video

Guitar Tabs 1

Guitar Tabs 2

Guitar Tabs 3

2. Strumming gallop:

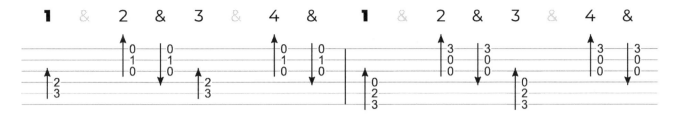

3. String fingerpicking - use the string fingerpicking pattern (**page 95**).
1 count - 1 pluck of a string.

1	-	2	-	3	-	4	-	**1**	-	2	-	3	-	4	-
Hush,		lit - tle ba		-		by,		don't		say a		word,			

```
|-----------------------------------|-----------------------------------|
|----------------------------1------|--------------------------------0--|
|------------------0----------------|-------------------------0---------|
|---------------2-------------------|----------------0------------------|
|--------3--------------------------|-----------------------------------|
|-----------------------------------|---------3-------------------------|
```

1	-	2	-	3	-	4	-	**1**	-	2	-	3	-	4	-
C				**C**				**G**				**G**			
Hush,		lit - tle ba		-		by,		don't		say a		word,			

1	-	2	-	3	-	4	-	**1**	-	2	-	3	-	4	-
G				**G**				**C**				**C**			
Mama's gonna		buy		you a		mock - ing		bird.		And					

1	-	2	-	3	-	4	-	**1**	-	2	-	3	-	4	-
C				**C**				**G**				**G**			
if		that		mock - ing		bird		don't		sing,					

1	-	2	-	3	-	4	-	**1**	-	2	-	3	-	4	-
G				**G**				**C**				**C**			
Mama's gonna		buy		you a		dia		-		mond		ring.			

HOME ON THE RANGE

Size **6/8**. The tempo is **60** beats per minute. In the size of 6/8 the organization of the bar consists of 3 lobes and for 1 beat of the metronome there are 3 counts with eighth notes. (Just as if you count 1-2-3 for every tick of second hand.

As in exercise 4.3. Exercise 8. Size 6/8. Counting with eighth notes **page 130**).

This song can be played in many ways:

1. Sliding the thumb down the strings on the 1st and 4th counts (i.e. every 3rd count)

2. Play strumming.

Lyrics

Oh, give me a home where the buffalo roam,
Where the deer and the antelope play;
Where seldom is heard a discouraging word
And the skies are not cloudy all day

Home, home on the range
Where the deer and the antelope play
Where seldom is heard a discouraging word
And the skies are not cloudy all day.

How often at night when the heavens are bright
With the lights from the glittering stars
Have I stood there amazed and asked as I gazed
If their glory exceeds that of ours.

1. Sliding your thumb down the strings on the 1st and 4th counts (i.e. every 3rd count):

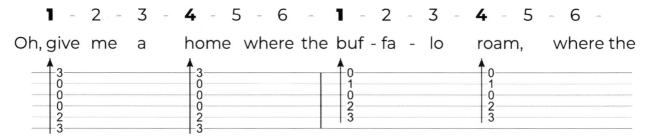

2. Strumming:

For convenience, size 6/8 can be counted instead of 1-2-3-4-5-6, **like this**: *1-2-3-1-2-3*

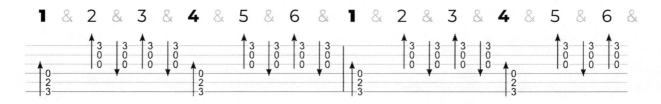

1 - 2 - 3 - 4 - 5 - 6 - **1** - 2 - 3 - 4 - 5 - 6 -
G　　　　　　　　**G**　　　　　**C**　　　　　**C**
Oh, give　me　a　　home　where the buf - fa - lo　　roam,　　where the

1 - 2 - 3 - 4 - 5 - 6 - **1** - 2 - 3 - 4 - 5 - 6 -
G　　　　　　　　**G**　　　　　**D**　　　　　**D**
deer　　and the an - te - lope play;　　　　　　where

1 - 2 - 3 - 4 - 5 - 6 - **1** - 2 - 3 - 4 - 5 - 6 -
G　　　　　　　　**G**　　　　　**C**　　　　　**C**
sel - dom is　　heard　　a dis-cour-a - ging word　　and the

1 - 2 - 3 - 4 - 5 - 6 - **1** - 2 - 3 - 4 - 5 - 6 -
G　　　　　　　　**D**　　　　　**G**　　　　　**G**
skies　are not　clou-dy　all　day.

1 - 2 - 3 - 4 - 5 - 6 - **1** - 2 - 3 - 4 - 5 - 6 -
D　　　　　　　　**D**　　　　　**G**　　　　　**G**
Home,　　　　home　on the　range　　　　　　where the

1 - 2 - 3 - 4 - 5 - 6 - **1** - 2 - 3 - 4 - 5 - 6 -
Em　　　　　　**A**　　　　　**D**　　　　　**D**
deer　　and the an - te - lope play;　　　　　　where

1 - 2 - 3 - 4 - 5 - 6 - **1** - 2 - 3 - 4 - 5 - 6 -
G　　　　　　　　**G**　　　　　**C**　　　　　**C**
sel - dom is　　heard　　a dis-cour-a - ging word　　and the

1 - 2 - 3 - 4 - 5 - 6 - **1** - 2 - 3 - 4 - 5 - 6 -
G　　　　　　　　**D**　　　　　**G**　　　　　**G**
skies　are not　clou-dy　all　day.

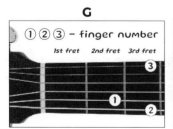

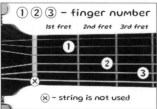

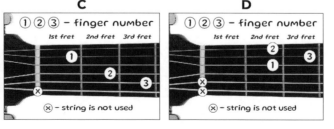

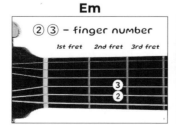

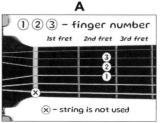

O HOLY NIGHT

Size **6/8**. The tempo is **100** beats per minute. In the size of 6/8 the organization of the bar consists of 3 lobes and for 1 beat of the metronome there are 3 counts with eighth notes. (Just as if you count 1-2-3 for every tick of the second hand. As in exercise 4.3. Exercise 8. Size 6/8. Counting with eighth notes **page 130**).

Lyrics

O Holy night! The stars are brightly shining
It is the night of our dear Savior's birth
Long lay the world in sin and error pining
'Til He appeared and the soul felt its worth.

CHORDS

G

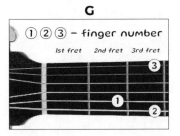

C

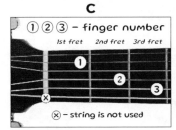

D

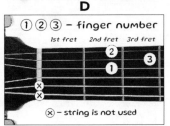

You can play this song by sliding your thumb down the strings for every 1st count.

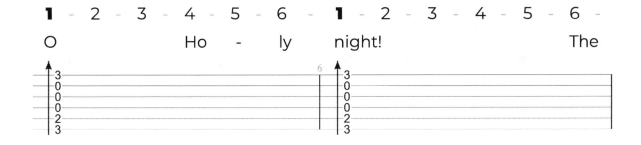

1 - 2 - 3 - 4 - 5 - 6 - **1** - 2 - 3 - 4 - 5 - 6 -
G   G
O   Ho - ly   night!   The

1 - 2 - 3 - 4 - 5 - 6 - **1** - 2 - 3 - 4 - 5 - 6 -
C   G
stars   are   bright - ly   shin   -   ing

1 - 2 - 3 - 4 - 5 - 6 - **1** - 2 - 3 - 4 - 5 - 6 -
G   G
It   is   the   night   of   our

1 - 2 - 3 - 4 - 5 - 6 - **1** - 2 - 3 - 4 - 5 - 6 -
D   G
de   -   ar   sav   -   ior's birth

1 - 2 - 3 - 4 - 5 - 6 - **1** - 2 - 3 - 4 - 5 - 6 -
G   G
Long   lay   the world   in

1 - 2 - 3 - 4 - 5 - 6 - **1** - 2 - 3 - 4 - 5 - 6 -
C   G
sin   and er   -   ror pin   -   ing

1 - 2 - 3 - 4 - 5 - 6 - **1** - 2 - 3 - 4 - 5 - 6 -
G   G
'Til   He   ap - peared   and   the

1 - 2 - 3 - 4 - 5 - 6 - **1** - 2 - 3 - 4 - 5 - 6 -
D   G
soul   felt   its   worth.

OH WHEN THE SAINTS

Size **4/4**. The tempo is **100** beats per minute. Each beat of the metronome will be 1/4. 4 beats of the metronome will equal 1 bar.

This song can be played in many ways:

1. Sliding the thumb down the strings for every 1st measure of the beat
2. Play the strumming down - up - dead note - up (which you practiced in chapter 3).

Lyrics

Oh when the saints
Go marching in
Oh when the saints go marching in
I want to be in that number
Oh when the saints go marching in

CHORDS

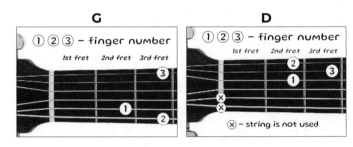

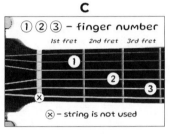

1. Sliding the thumb down the strings for every 1st measure of the beat:

Oh when the

1 　 2 　 3 　 4 　 **1** 　 2 　 3 　 4

saints. 　　　 Go marching in. 　　　　 Oh when the

```
3------------------|3---------------
0------------------|0---------------
0------------------|0---------------
0------------------|0---------------
2------------------|2---------------
3------------------|3---------------
```

Video

Guitar Tabs 1

Guitar Tabs 2

2. Strumming (down - up - dead note - up):

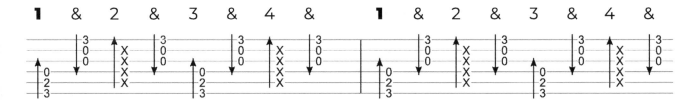

Oh when the

1	-	2	-	3	-	4	-	1	-	2	-	3	-	4	-
G								**G**							
saints.						Go	marching in.					Oh	when the		

1	-	2	-	3	-	4	-	1	-	2	-	3	-	4	-
G								**D**							
saints		go		march -	ing		in.					I	want to		

1	-	2	-	3	-	4	-	1	-	2	-	3	-	4	-
G								**C**							
be				in		that		number.				Oh	when the		

1	-	2	-	3	-	4	-	1	-	2	-	3	-	4	-
G				**D**				**G**							
saints		go		march -	ing		in.								

RED RIVER VALLEY

Size **4/4**. The tempo is **130** beats per minute. Each beat of the metronome will be 1/4. 4 beats of the metronome will equal 1 bar.

This song can be played in many ways:
1. Sliding the thumb down the strings for every 1st beat count
2. Play the strumming gallop "down - *skip* - dead note - up" (the same strumming as in "5.4. Exercise 2")
3. Play the strumming gallop (same as the previous variation, but without the "dead note").

Lyrics
From this valley they say you are going,
We will miss your bright eyes and sweet smile,
For they say you are taking the sunshine
Which has brightened our pathways a while.

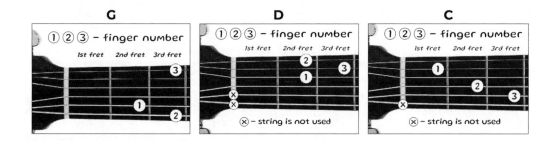

1. Sliding your thumb down the strings for every 1st measure of the beat:

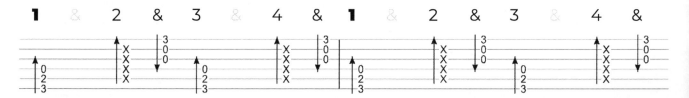

2. Strumming gallop "down - *skip***- dead note - up":**

Video

Guitar Tabs 1

Guitar Tabs 2

Guitar Tabs 3

3. Strumming gallop:

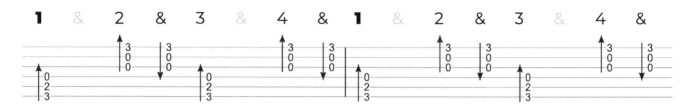

1	&	2	&	3	&	4	&	**1**	&	2	&	3	&	4	&

From   this

1	-	2	-	3	-	4	-	**1**	-	2	-	3	-	4	-
G								**G**							

val   -   ley   they   say   you   are

1	-	2	-	3	-	4	-	**1**	-	2	-	3	-	4	-
G								**G**							

go   -   ing.   We   will

1	-	2	-	3	-	4	-	**1**	-	2	-	3	-	4	-
G								**G**							

miss   your   bright   eyes   and   sweet

1	-	2	-	3	-	4	-	**1**	-	2	-	3	-	4	-
D								**D**							

smile.   For   they

1	-	2	-	3	-	4	-	**1**	-	2	-	3	-	4	-
G								**G**							

say   you   are   tak   -   ing   the

1	-	2	-	3	-	4	-	**1**	-	2	-	3	-	4	-
C								**C**							

sun   -   shine.   Which   has

1	-	2	-	3	-	4	-	**1**	-	2	-	3	-	4	-
G								**D**							

bright   -   ened   our   path   -   ways   a

1	-	2	-	3	-	4	-	**1**	-	2	-	3	-	4	-
G								**G**							

while.

SKIP TO MY LOU

Size **4/4**. The tempo is **120** beats per minute. Each beat of the metronome will be 1/4. 4 beats of the metronome will equal 1 bar.

This song can be played in many ways:
1. Sliding the thumb down the strings on the 1st and 3rd count of the measure
2. Play a strumming gallop.

Lyrics
Flies in the buttermilk, shoo fly shoo
Flies in the buttermilk, shoo fly shoo
Flies in the buttermilk, shoo fly shoo
Skip to my Lou, my darling

Lou, Lou, skip to my Lou
Lou, Lou, skip to my Lou
Lou, Lou, skip to my Lou
Skip to my Lou, my darling

CHORDS

G

① ② ③ – finger number
1st fret   2nd fret   3rd fret

D

① ② ③ – finger number
1st fret   2nd fret   3rd fret

ⓧ – string is not used

1. Sliding your thumb down the strings for every 1st measure of the beat:

1	2	**3**	4	**1**	2	**3**	4
Flies	in	the but-ter - milk,		shoo	fly	shoo	

```
3           3           3           3
0           0           0           0
0           0           0           0
0           0           0           0
2           2           2           2
3           3           3           3
```

Video

Guitar Tabs 1

Guitar Tabs 2

2. Strumming gallop:

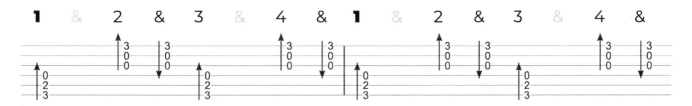

1	-	2	-	3	-	4	-	**1**	-	2	-	3	-	4	-
G				G				G				G			
Flies		in		the but-ter-milk,				shoo		fly		shoo			

1	-	2	-	3	-	4	-	**1**	-	2	-	3	-	4	-
D				D				D				D			
Flies		in		the but-ter-milk,				shoo		fly		shoo			

1	-	2	-	3	-	4	-	**1**	-	2	-	3	-	4	-
G				G				G				G			
Flies		in		the but-ter-milk,				shoo		fly		shoo			

1	-	2	-	3	-	4	-	**1**	-	2	-	3	-	4	-
D				D				G				G			
Skip		to		my Lou,		my		dar		-		ling			

1	-	2	-	3	-	4	-	**1**	-	2	-	3	-	4	-
G				G				G				G			
Lou,				Lou,				skip		to		my Lou			

1	-	2	-	3	-	4	-	**1**	-	2	-	3	-	4	-
D				D				D				D			
Lou,				Lou,				skip		to		my Lou			

1	-	2	-	3	-	4	-	**1**	-	2	-	3	-	4	-
G				G				G				G			
Lou,				Lou,				skip		to		my Lou			

1	-	2	-	3	-	4	-	**1**	-	2	-	3	-	4	-
D				D				G				G			
Skip		to		my Lou,		my		dar		-		ling			

MY COUNTRY TIS OF THEE

Size **3/4**. The tempo is **120** beats per minute. 3 beats of the metronome will equal 1 bar.

Lyrics
My country, 'tis of thee
Sweet land of liberty
Of thee I sing;
Land where my fathers died
Land of the pilgrims' pride
From ev'ry mountainside
Let freedom ring!

You can play this song by running your thumb down the strings on the 1st beat of the measure.

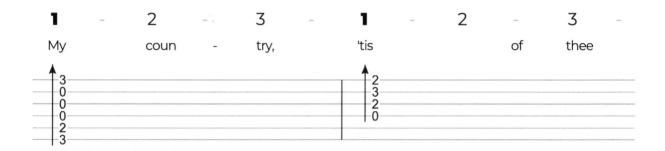

CHORDS

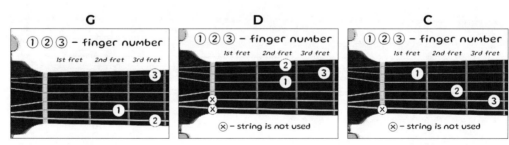

1	-	2	-	3	-	**1**	-	2	-	3	-
G						D					
My		coun	-	try,		'tis				of	thee

1	-	2	-	3	-	**1**	-	2	-	3	-
G						G					
Sweet		land		of		lib		-		er	- ty

1	-	2	-	3	-	**1**	-	2	-	3	-
D						G					
Of		thee		I		sing;					

1	-	2	-	3	-	**1**	-	2	-	3	-
G						G					
Land		where	-	my		fa		-		thers died	

1	-	2	-	3	-	**1**	-	2	-	3	-
D						D					
Land		of		the		pil		-		grims' pride	

1	-	2	-	3	-	**1**	-	2	-	3	-
G						G					
From		ev'	-	ry		moun		-		tain - side	

1	-	2	-	3	-	**1**	-	2	-	3	-
C						G					
Let		free	-	dom		ring!					

THE FIRST NOEL

Size **3/4**. The tempo is **115** beats per minute. Each beat of the metronome will be 1/4. 3 beats of the metronome will equal 1 bar.

Lyrics
The first Noel, the Angel did say
Was to certain poor shepherds in fields as they lay
In fields where they lay keeping their sheep
On a cold winter night that was so deep.
Noel, Noel, Noel, Noel
Born is the King of Israel!

You can play this song by sliding your thumb down the strings for 1st beat:

1	-	2	-	3	-	**1**	-	2	-	3	-
The	first			No	-	el					

```
    |  2                   |  0
    |  3                   |  2
    |  2                   |  2
    |  0                   |  2
    |                      |  0
```

CHORDS

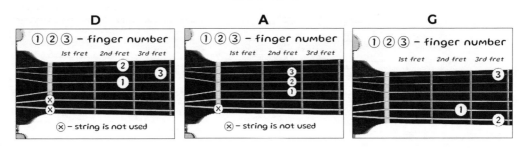

D   A   G

① ② ③ – finger number

1st fret   2nd fret   3rd fret

ⓧ – string is not used

1	-	2	-	3	-	**1**	-	2	-	3	-
D						A					
The first				No	-	el,				the	

1	-	2	-	3	-	**1**	-	2	-	3	-
G						D					
An	-	gel		did		say.				Was	to

1	-	2	-	3	-	**1**	-	2	-	3	-
G						D					
cer	-	tain		poor		shep	-	herds		in	

1	-	2	-	3	-	**1**	-	2	-	3	-
D						G		D			
fields		as		they		lay.				In	

1	-	2	-	3	-	**1**	-	2	-	3	-
D						A					
Fields				where		they				lay	

1	-	2	-	3	-	**1**	-	2	-	3	-
G						D					
keep	-	ing		their		sheep.				On	a

1	-	2	-	3	-	**1**	-	2	-	3	-
G						D					
cold		win	-	ter		night				that	

1	-	2	-	3	-	**1**	-	2	-	3	-
D				G		D					
was				so		deep.				No	-

1	-	2	-	3	-	**1**	-	2	-	3	-
D						A					
el,				No	-	el,				No	-

1	-	2	-	3	-	**1**	-	2	-	3	-
G						D					
el,				No	-	el.					

1	-	2	-	3	-	**1**	-	2	-	3	-
G						D					
Born		is		the		King				of	

1	-	2	-	3	-	**1**	-	2	-	3	-
D				G		D					
Is		-		ra	-	el.					

Barre Chords

The barre chord technique allows you to play a large number of chords in any part of the neck of the guitar.

The chords we've studied so far are open chords. Open chords are chords that use at least one open (unstrummed) string and are placed at the headstock of the neck on the 1st, 2nd and 3rd fret.

There are VERY many different chords that can be placed with a barre chord. For example, let's count open chords (we'll only count simple chord forms. E, Em, G, A, Am, C, Dm, D - you get a total of 8 open chords. Barre chords can be set as many as open chords + about 20 other chords.

Barre chords can easily replace open chords, but open chords cannot replace barre chords.

If you skip the topic of practicing barre chords, you will lose about 90% of the possibilities of playing chords on guitar and playing songs in other tonalities that use barre chords. Let's take the song "Greensleeves" as an example. It uses 6 chords, 5 of which are open chords and 1 barre chord (F chord). If you skip learning how to play barre chord, you will not be able to play "Greensleeves".

What the barre chord does?

The basic essence of a barre chord is to imitate the guitar's metal strip with your index finger. Let's take the E chord as an example. Look at its shape.

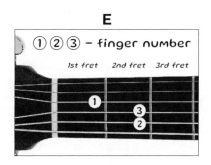

Since the metal strip on our guitar acts as the 0 fret, we don't need to clamp anything on the open strings in chord E. It turns out that only 3 fingers are involved in setting the E chord. If we move the E chord figure 1 fret to the right, then we need to press 6 notes in some way. Which is physically impossible, because there are 5 fingers on the hand. But if we use the index finger as an imitation of a metal strip, i.e. press all 6 strings with it, then it becomes possible to put the same chord figure as E. That's the whole essence of the barre technique.

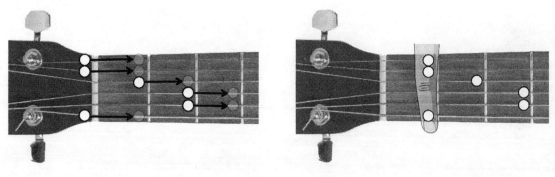

In this technique, the thumb of the left hand is moved to a different position, not on top of the neck, but at the back at the top of the neck, approximately opposite the index finger. The thumb can be turned slightly to the left for convenience, if necessary. The thumb is fully straightened and rests near the joint, with the inside of the thumb.

Basic Peculiarities of Barre Chord Progressions

1. The thumb should be placed with the pad of the finger behind the fingerboard.

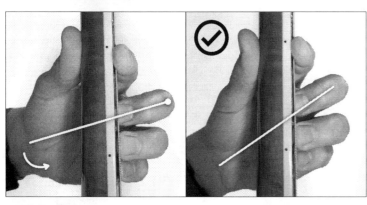

2. To place the barre chord, turn the left hand counterclockwise on the axis by about 10-20 degrees. *This should be done to make it more comfortable to grip the strings with your fingers.*

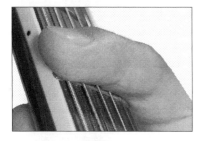

3. Put the index finger just behind the metal fret strip, so that the strip touches the right side of the index finger, or put a little on top of the metal strip. The criterion is that the strings should not be muted, but sounded.

4. The index finger is shaped like an arc - this is to make the hand comfortable.

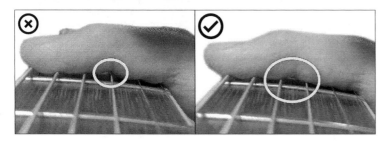

5. The bends of the phalanges of the index finger should be between the strings. *If these bends fall on the string, it will be more difficult or impossible to clamp these strings because the string "falls through" the bend of the finger.*

In order to master a full 6-string barre chord you need to master barre chord on 2 strings, then on 3, then on 4, then on 5 strings and then on 6 strings.

5.5 Exercise 1

Mini Barre Chord on 2 strings (1st and 2nd)

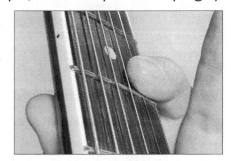

- Place your left thumb behind the neck opposite the **3rd** fret
- Turn your left hand 10-20 degrees to the left (*like step 1, 2 on the previous page*).

1. Place your index finger on the 1st and 2nd strings on the 3rd fret just behind the metal fret strip.
2. Check the sound of the 1st and 2nd strings. They should sound even (no rattling). If the strings sound bad, check how your index finger rests according to the instructions.
3. Remove your index finger and repeat **step 1**.

Play this exercise on different frets. Place your index finger on the 1st, 2nd, 3rd, 4th, 5th, 6th, 7th fret.

5.5 Exercise 2

Mini Barre Chord on 3 strings (1, 2, 3 strings)

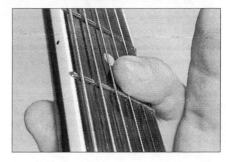

Same as the previous exercise, but place your index finger on the 1st, 2nd and 3rd strings.

Also play this exercise on different frets. (1-7).

5.5 Exercise 3

4-string barre chord (1, 2, 3, 4 strings)

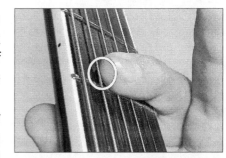

- Place your left thumb behind the neck opposite the **3rd** fret
- Turn your left hand 10-20 degrees to the left (*like step 1, 2 on the previous page*).

1. Put your index finger on the 1st, 2nd, 3rd and 4th strings on the 3rd fret just behind the metal fret strip. This is where we add a new detail. The tip of your index finger should touch the 5th string to deaden it!
2. Check the sound of the 1st through 4th strings. They should sound even (no rattling). Also check if the 5th string sounds. If it does, place your index finger a little higher so that it muffles the 5th string with its tip.
3. Remove your index finger and repeat **step 1**.

Play this exercise on different frets (1-7).
P.S. It is less easy to barre chord on the 1st fret because of the higher string tension at the zero fret.

5.5 Exercise 4

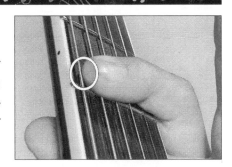

5-string barre chord (1st, 2nd, 3rd, 4th, 5th strings)

The same as the previous exercise, but place your index finger on the 5th string and touch the 6th string with your fingertip to muffle it. Notice that the more strings you jam with your index finger, the more your index finger takes on an arched shape.

Play this exercise on different frets (1-7).
P.S. It is less easy to barre chord on the 1st fret because of the greater string tension at the zero fret.

5.5 Exercise 5

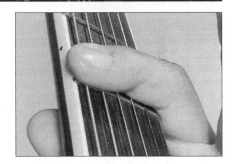

Full Barre Chord

Now put your index finger on all six strings.

Play this exercise on different frets (1-7).

5.5 Exercise 6

A barre chord

You have already practiced the A chord, but it was an open chord on the 5th string. You can also play this chord on the 6th string, but you will need a barre chord technique.
Now that you've mastered the index finger placement for barre chord, let's do a real barre chord.
(continued on next page)

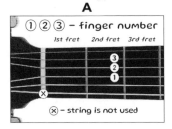

A

① ② ③ – finger number
1st fret   2nd fret   3rd fret

ⓧ – string is not used

1. Place your index finger on all 6 strings on the 5th fret, just behind the metal strip on the 5th fret.
2. Place the tip of your ring finger on the 5th string at the 7th fret.
3. Put the tip of your pinky finger on the 4th string at the 7th fret.
4. Put the tip of your middle finger on the 3rd string at the 6th fret.
5. Check the sound of the chord:
   - If the 1st, 2nd or 6th strings are not sounding, check the placement of your index finger.
   - If the 5th string doesn't sound, check your ring finger to see if it's holding the string?
   - If the 4th string doesn't sound, check the pinky finger to see if it is pressing the string?
   - If the 3rd string doesn't sound, check your middle finger to see if it's pressing the string? Also check if your pinky finger is touching the 4th string?

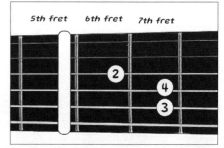

A barre

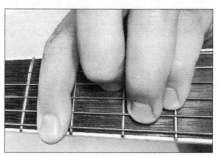

IMPORTANT, for easy memorization of new chords, use the technique in 2.3.1 "How to quickly learn chord placement and how to practice exercises 14-25" (p.88).

For interest, you can compare the sound of an A chord on the open 5th string and an A chord with a barre chord on the 6th string.

You need to practice setting chords with barre chords. When you've set 100+ times, you'll be able to set almost any barre chord at once and then you'll be able to play any song at all.

Now you can practice playing a song like "**Buffalo Gals** (p.146)" using not an open A chord, but an A chord with a barre chord.

5.5 Exercise 7

Dm barre chord

Remember the Dm chord from the 4th string?

It can also be played with a barre chord from the 5th string. Note that the figure of the Dm chord from the 5th string coincides completely with the figure of the A chord from the 6th string. Why this happens, and why the same chords can be placed in different places on the guitar, will be discussed in the next book.

Dm (open)

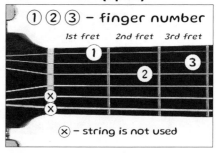

① ② ③ – finger number

1st fret 2nd fret 3rd fret

ⓧ – string is not used

Dm barre

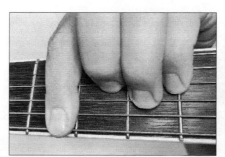

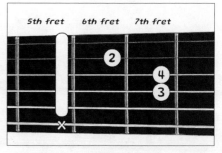

🎓 5.5 Exercise 8

F chord

This chord will greatly expand the arsenal of songs you can play. It will be used in some of the songs in this book, "Silent Night", "Shenandoah" and "Greensleeves". The shape of the F chord is exactly the same as the A barre chord. Only it's not placed on the 5th fret, but on the 1st fret.

I'll tell you the good news, the shape of the barre chord will always be the same, which is why you can put any chord you want. If you move the F chord to the 3rd fret, it will be a G chord, which you already know, only it will be a variation of the G barre chord. Or if you move the F chord to the 7th fret, it's a B chord.

F chord placement:

1. Place your index finger on all 6 strings on the 1st fret, just behind the metal strip on the 1st fret, and place your thumb behind the neck.
2. Place the tip of your ring finger on the 5th string at the 3rd fret.
3. Put the tip of your little finger on the 4th string at the 3rd fret.
4. Tip of the middle finger on the 3rd string at the 2nd fret.
5. Check the sound of the chord:

   - If the 1st, 2nd or 6th strings are not sounding, check the placement of your index finger.
   - If the 5th string doesn't sound, check your ring finger to see if it's holding the string?
   - If the 4th string doesn't sound, check the pinky finger to see if it is pressing the string?
   - If the 3rd string doesn't sound, check your middle finger to see if it's pressing the string? Also check if your pinky finger is touching the 4th string?

P.S. For easy memorization of new chords, use the technique in 2.3.1 "How to quickly learn chord placement and how to practice exercises 14-25" (p.88).

When you have mastered the F chord progression, move on to playing the songs below.

SILENT NIGHT

Size **3/4**. The tempo is **120** beats per minute. Each beat of the metronome will be 1/4. 3 beats of the metronome will equal 1 bar.

Lyrics
Silent night, holy night
All is calm, all is bright
Round yon Virgin, Mother and Child
Holy Infant so tender and mild
Sleep in heavenly peace
Sleep in heavenly peace.

You can play this song by sliding your thumb down the strings for 1st beat:

1	2	3	**1**	2	3
Si	-	lent	night,		

```
    0              0
    1              1
    0              0
    2              2
    3              3
```

CHORDS

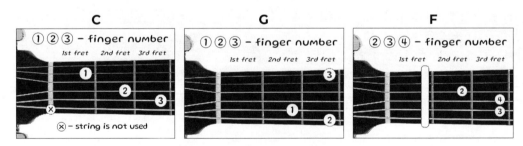

C — ①②③ – finger number — 1st fret, 2nd fret, 3rd fret — ⊗ – string is not used

G — ①②③ – finger number — 1st fret, 2nd fret, 3rd fret

F — ②③④ – finger number — 1st fret, 2nd fret, 3rd fret

Video

Guitar Tabs

1 C	-	2	-	3	-	**1** C	-	2	-	3	-
Si	-			lent		night,					

1 C	-	2	-	3	-	**1** C	-	2	-	3	-
Ho	-			ly		night,					

1 G	-	2	-	3	-	**1** G	-	2	-	3	-
All				is		calm,					

1 C	-	2	-	3	-	**1** C	-	2	-	3	-
All				is		bright.					

1 F	-	2	-	3	-	**1** F	-	2	-	3	-
Round				yon		Vir	-			gin	

1 C	-	2	-	3	-	**1** C	-	2	-	3	-
Moth	-	er	and			Child					

1 F	-	2	-	3	-	**1** F	-	2	-	3	-
Ho	-		ly			In	-		fant	so	

1 C	-	2	-	3	-	**1** C	-	2	-	3	-
ten	-	der	and			mild					

1 G	-	2	-	3	-	**1** G	-	2	-	3	-
Sleep			in			heav	-	en - ly			

1 C	-	2	-	3	-	**1** C	-	2	-	3	-
peace											

1 C	-	2	-	3	-	**1** G	-	2	-	3	-
Sle	-	ep	in			heav	-	en - ly			

1 C	-	2	-	3	-	**1** C	-	2	-	3	-
peace.											

SHENANDOAH

Size **4/4**. The tempo is **90** beats per minute. Each beat of the metronome will be 1/4. 4 beats of the metronome will equal 1 bar.

This song can be played in many ways:
1. Sliding the thumb down the strings on the 1st and 3rd count of a measure.
2. Play the strumming gallop "down - *skip* - dead note - up" (the same strumming as in "5.4. Exercise 2").

Lyrics
Oh Shenandoah, I long to hear you,
Away, you rolling river.
Oh Shenandoah, I long to hear you,
Away, we're bound away
Cross the wide Missouri.

1. Sliding the thumb down the strings on the 1st and 3rd counts of a measure:

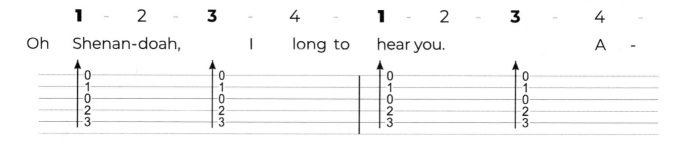

2. Strumming gallop "down - skip - dead note - up":

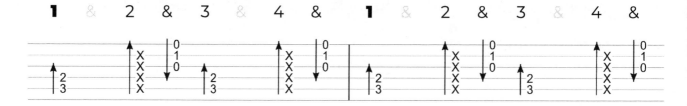

Video

Guitar Tabs 1

Guitar Tabs 2

1	-	2	-	3	-	4	-	**1**	-	2	-	3	-	4	-
C						**C**		**C**						**C**	
Oh Shenan-doah,				I		long to	hear you.							A	-

1	-	2	-	3	-	4	-	**1**	-	2	-	3	-	4	-
F				**F**				**C**						**C**	
way				you roll-ing riv - er.										Oh	

1	-	2	-	3	-	4	-	**1**	-	2	-	3	-	4	-
Am				**Am**				**F**				**F**			
Shenan-doah,				I		long to	hear you.							A	-

1	-	2	-	3	-	4	-	**1**	-	2	-	3	-	4	-
C				**C**				**Em**				**Am**			
way				we're bound		away							Cross tthe		

1	-	2	-	3	-	4	-	**1**	-	2	-	3	-	4	-
F				**F**		**G**		**C**							
wide				Mis-sou		-	ri.								

CHORDS

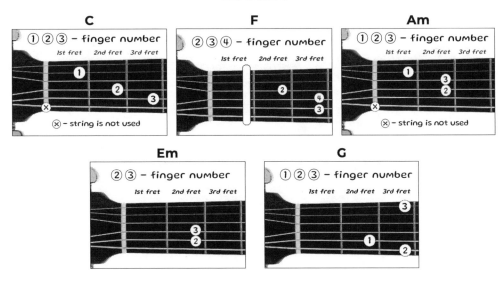

GREENSLEEVES

Size **6/8**. The tempo is **70** beats per minute. In the size of 6/8 the organization of the bar consists of 3 lobes and for 1 beat of the metronome there are 3 counts with 8 notes. (Just as if you count 1-2-3 for every tick of the second hand.

As in exercise 4.3. Exercise 8. Size 6/8. Counting with eighth notes **page 130**).

This song can be played in many ways, but at your current level it is best played by simply sliding your thumb down the strings on the 1st and 4th counts (i.e. every 3rd count).

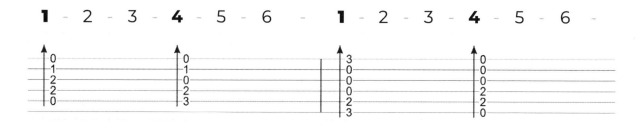

CHORDS

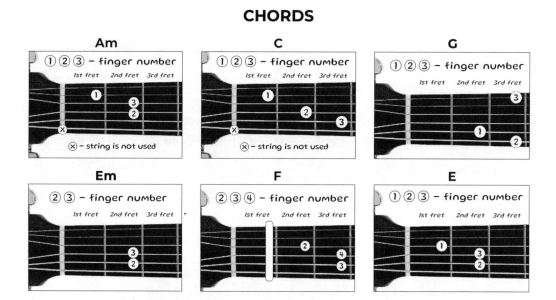

Video

Guitar Tabs

1 - 2 - 3 - 4 - 5 - 6 - **1** - 2 - 3 - 4 - 5 - 6 -
Am   C   G   Em

1 - 2 - 3 - 4 - 5 - 6 - **1** - 2 - 3 - 4 - 5 - 6 -
Am   F   E   E

1 - 2 - 3 - 4 - 5 - 6 - **1** - 2 - 3 - 4 - 5 - 6 -
Am   C   G   Em

1 - 2 - 3 - 4 - 5 - 6 - **1** - 2 - 3 - 4 - 5 - 6 -
Am   E   Am   Am

1 - 2 - 3 - 4 - 5 - 6 - **1** - 2 - 3 - 4 - 5 - 6 -
C   C   G   Em

1 - 2 - 3 - 4 - 5 - 6 - **1** - 2 - 3 - 4 - 5 - 6 -
Am   F   E   E

1 - 2 - 3 - 4 - 5 - 6 - **1** - 2 - 3 - 4 - 5 - 6 -
C   C   G   Em

1 - 2 - 3 - 4 - 5 - 6 - **1** - 2 - 3 - 4 - 5 - 6 -
Am   E   Am   Am

WE WISH YOU A MERRY CHRISTMAS

Size **3/4**. The tempo is **140** beats per minute. Each beat of the metronome will be 1/4. 3 beats of the metronome will equal 1 bar.

This song can be played in many ways:
1. Sliding the thumb down the strings on the 1st counts.
2. Play strumming.

Lyrics
We wish you a merry Christmas,
We wish you a merry Christmas,
We wish you a merry Christmas
And a happy New Year.

Good tidings we bring
To you and your kin;
We wish you a merry Christmas
And a happy New Year!

1. Sliding the thumb down the strings on the 1st counts:

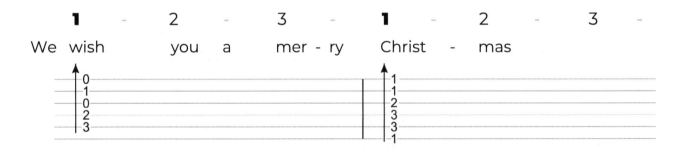

2. Play strumming:

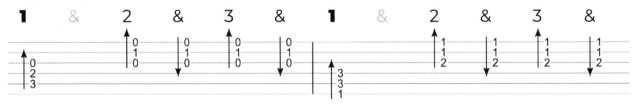

Video

Guitar Tabs 1

Guitar Tabs 2

1 C	-	2	-	3	-	**1** F	-	2	-	3	-
We wish		you	a	mer - ry		Christ	-	mas,		we	

1 D	-	2	-	3	-	**1** G	-	2	-	3	-
wish		you	a	mer - ry		Christ	-	mas,		we	

1 E	-	2	-	3	-	**1** Am	-	2	-	3	-
wish		you	a	mer - ry		Christ	-	mas,		and a	

1 F	-	2	-	3 G	-	**1** C	-	2	-	3	-
hap	-	py		New		Year.				Good	

1 C	-	2	-	3	-	**1** G	-	2	-	3	-
tid	-	ings		we		bring,				to	

1 Am	-	2	-	3	-	**1** G	-	2	-	3	-
you		and		your		kin.				We	

1 C	-	2	-	3	-	**1** Em	-	2	-	3	-
wish		you	a	mer - ry		Christ	-	mas,		and a	

1 F	-	2	-	3 G	-	**1** C	-	2	-	3	-
hap	-	py		New		Year.					

CHORDS

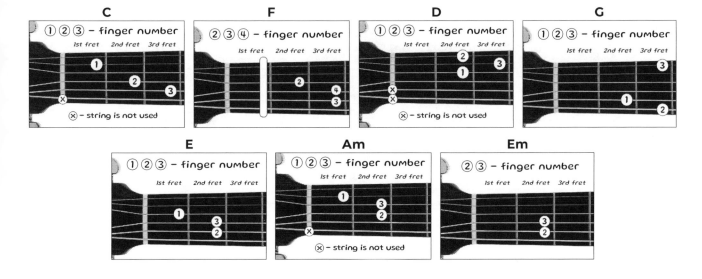

I hope you've played guitar for at least 30 hours total, following all of my recommendations and have already gotten a great result.

Book Review

Why would you leave a review on amazon about this book? There are 5 reasons, like the 5 fingers on your hand, like the 5 spurs on a starfish, like the 5 rings of the Olympics.

1. Self-reflection

When you describe in the review:

    a. what you have learned, what playing techniques you have practiced
    b. how easy and clear it was for you to learn from this book
    c. what songs you learned
    d. what cool emotions you experienced in the process of learning
    e. what good things you got from playing the guitar,

you will be able to self-reflect on the work you have done in your training, so that you can be happy for yourself about how well you have done in this interesting task.

2. Quality and detail of training materials

Imagine, or even remember, as if you bought another book. How much the other book explains everything abstractly and poorly. It's like, "sit like this and put your hand like this." You end up with bullshit because you don't understand anything. You have already seen for yourself how in this book in each of the 5 chapters, everything is written in detail and understandable, how much it is convenient and speeds up learning.

3. Helping other people

You'll also help other people just like you make the right decision by choosing this book to learn. Thousands of people will get a thrill out of playing guitar. Imagine how disappointed those people will be if they buy some other book that explains everything in the abstract. They'll think that playing guitar is really hard and they'll quit. Although playing guitar is cool, fun and easy!

4. Feedback for me, the author of this book

I want to be happy for your progress because I've worked hard to make the best guitar instruction book for you and I'd love to see your review on Amazon.

5. There will be more musicians in the world

Well, and the most important, FIFTH reason. By writing a review on Amazon about your great results of learning from this book you will increase the number of guitarists and happy people in this world!

Go to the QR code, rate this book and write in detail in the review, what you learned, what techniques of playing you practiced, how easy and clear it was for you to learn from this book?

Made in United States
Troutdale, OR
12/02/2024